CYBER PR®

FOR MUSICIANS

Tools, Tricks & Tactics for
Building Your Social Media House

CYBER PR®

FOR MUSICIANS

*Tools, Tricks & Tactics for
Building Your Social Media House*

Ariel Hyatt

2012
HUNTERCAT PRESS
New York

For Erskine.

TABLE OF CONTENTS

FOREWORD
by Bobby Owsinski

Over the last few years, I've given talks and presentations at colleges and conferences all over the world, and when speaking to artists and bands regarding social media, there are always two major complaints that pop up:

1. "Ugh, it takes so much time!"

2. "I'm doing it, and it isn't working!"

Once I've looked closely at a client's online strategy, what becomes most apparent is not that they're doing it "wrong," but that they have an incomplete picture of exactly what it is they're supposed to do. There are a lot of half-hearted forays into the different areas of social media with only limited execution. As a result, they have to spend a lot of time being "social," but they only receive a mediocre outcome.

If this is you, you're in for a revelation.

Cyber PR® For Musicians is the most complete roadmap to online success available today. It's easy to follow, and provides painless step-by-step instructions in every major facet of social media needed by an artist living in our current Music 3.0 world. Heck, I know this stuff and even I learned a lot! Trust me, you're not going to find a more complete approach in one place on how to make social media work for you.

Here's the catch. If you want an online strategy that really works, you have to spend the time to not only set it up properly, but also to continually feed the beast with content. Setting everything up takes some thought, but Ariel and her Cyber PR® team (the most cutting-edge and highly respected in the music business) lays it out in such a step-by-step approach that you'll be done before you know it. Generating content should be the fun part, and this book will even guide you with that. You just have to remember to do it.

By the way, you've no doubt read the interviews with various experts that always say how your music has got to be great first before any of this information can work. What they don't tell you is that "great" means different things to different people. One of the best features of the Internet is that it provides you with an opportunity to connect with a group of people that will love your music if only they can find you, and you can find them. The group may or may not be large, but they'll be your fans for life if you let them. If you follow the outline in Cyber PR® for Musicians, you are not one, but many steps closer to making that happen.

BOBBY OWSINSKI, Fall 2012

Bobby Owsinski's 15 bestselling books and video courses have become an essential ingredient for every home or commercial recording studio, musician, engineer, and band.

INTRODUCTION

A. THE FOUNDATION OF YOUR SOCIAL MEDIA HOUSE

- 7 of the top 10 most followed Twitter users are musicians

- 51% of music in the UK is found via search engines

- Pandora streamed 13 billion hours of music in 2012

- 9 of the top 10 most liked people on Facebook are musicians

- VEVO streams 4 billion music videos per month

- Over 1 billion music playlists have been created on Spotify

- Music download sites account for 70% of global digital revenue

'm really proud of you for buying this book! I don't mean that statement in an arrogant or snarky way; it's just that I've spent my entire adult life and career marketing and promoting artists and I've learned a lot of things I can't wait to teach you.

What follows is as close as you can get to experiencing a blueprint for Cyber PR®, a brand and system I created and continue to co-create with my incredible team.

The Cyber PR® process marks the intersection of social media with engaged behavior, PR, and online marketing. And I almost burst with pride when I share that Cyber PR® is the name and backbone of two courses taught at a top music business university (both intro and advanced courses).

Since I dove into the online marketing world, I have made it my mission to educate artists on how to take advantage of all of the tools and tricks available to them. I've been invited to speak at festivals and conferences in 12 countries and I continue to passionately explore and share what I keep learning because it not only keeps my agency going, it also makes a difference for artists.

B. LET'S START WITH YOUR OBJECTIONS

(I Know You Have Them!)

Once upon a time, I found myself chatting with a perfect stranger at a music conference in Australia. It turns out, he was a well-known musician with quite a few top 10 hits. Noting my foreign accent he asked, "What brings you here?"

"I teach artists about online marketing and social media," I answered, sheepishly (because this fact is not always met with elated enthusiasm).

"Really?" he said.

"Yes, *really.*" I responded.

He asked, "You know one thing I've noticed about social media?"

"What is that?" I was interested to hear what he would say.

He told me, "I've noticed that you don't really have to be a great artist or well respected by your musician peers to succeed nowadays. You just have to be really good at marketing, and you will get more success than you ever would have in the past."

He's right, in one sense. I'm not saying that his point is fair, but he voiced what 99 percent of most artists really think: *That guy's music sucks, but he's good at being pushy on Facebook, so he gets more people to his gigs than me, and he has more success than I do.*

Really? Is that what you think?

It doesn't matter if you think that artist sucks. The point is, he managed to identify and relate to enough people who think his music is great, and those people respond to him and reward him for his efforts.

I invite you to stop judging others and worry about how to make a difference for yourself. Why? Because there are a billion people to connect with on Facebook alone.

Anyone can connect with a few hundred people, forge great relationships and market to a tribe of fans who will love you. Simple. What is not simple is getting your judgments about yourself and other artists out of the way and just diving in and learning.

I am here to debunk a few of your *ahem* resistances, and the aforementioned story of my conversation in Australia takes us to #1 on the list of ...

C. TOP SEVEN REASONS ARTISTS STRONGLY RESIST SOCIAL MEDIA

1. "I don't want to be pushy and over-hype-y like all those other artists that I hate."

I know, *talking* about yourself is icky. But having people *respond* to you is wonderful. My advice is: when you use social media, take the spotlight off yourself and shine it on others (the people in your community, fans, and friends). *This is a theme that will run throughout this book.*

Share things. Don't even think of marketing yourself or your music for a few months until you get the hang of it. After you do, use it to gently lead people to your newsletter sign-up, your website, and to help yourself with Google rankings.

Keep this in mind: According to a 2012 study by Socialnomics.net, 78 percent of people trust peer recommendations (i.e. the "Like" button on Facebook) for products and services that they *buy*. Only 14 percent trust TV, radio, and print advertising. In other words, you need to be an artist that peers are recommending.

2. "Promoting my music on social media won't put any money in my pocket. I've tried it, and it just creates more work for me."

Social media and ROI (return on investment) are hard to tie together. Social media use most likely won't directly put money in your pocket in the short term. But, when used in connection with traditional marketing, and as part of a master plan, social media is integral in reinforcing relationships between you and your fans. Down the line, that can lead them to a point of purchase, particularly if you know how to ask. Google rankings and your email newsletter list will be two vital components to putting money in your pocket, and social media can help you strengthen both of them.

3. *"Social media and marketing take too much time. I only want to be 'an artist' playing my music."*

Being successful does (and will) take hard work and always has. Here are a few personal questions to consider: How much time are you willing to commit to learning new skills and tools?

If the answer is, "None. I just want to play," that's okay. I have worked with many artists who are pushing and forcing themselves to "succeed" without looking at what success really means to them.

My friend, Derek Sivers (the founder of CD Baby), wrote the most powerful blog post I have ever read on the artist dilemma when it comes to success vs. creativity. This just might convince you to think making music for profit may not be for you. In it he says:

> "When someone creates something that is really important, powerful, and valuable to them, it's hard to imagine that it's not important, powerful, and valuable to others.... But money only comes from doing something valuable to others.... If you stop expecting your art to be valuable to anyone but you, your conflicted mind can

finally be at peace. Do it only because you love it, and it honestly doesn't matter what anyone else thinks.... You'll probably be happier with your art because of this change in mindset. Ironically, others may appreciate it more too, though you honestly won't care. Stop expecting it to be valuable to others. Accept it as personal and precious to only you. Get your money elsewhere."

- Derek Sivers

In my philosophy, there's an in-between value that Derek does not assign, and it's not so black and white. That value is: How you touch and inspire people along your journey of sharing your art may not have a high financial value at all. It may be deeply satisfying for you to take 10, 50, or 200 friends along your creative journey.

4. "Social media isn't 'real' media. It has no impact on the 'real' world."

Citizen journalists are the new influencers. They include bloggers, podcasters, Internet radio stations, and people with large followings on social media sites. If you doubt their influence, take a good, long look at traditional media these days: approximately once every minute, TV news broadcasts direct you to their Twitter and Facebook pages. Many of them have a permanent graphic on the screen with Facebook and Twitter feeds (think of 24-hour news channels like CNN or MSNBC). The "real" media is constantly telling viewers to go to social media and contribute. And note: There are over 200 million blogs online. I'll bet my life that one or two of them may just want to write about you.

5. "Social media is just for young people. I'm not in 'that' generation."

Think again: The average age of Twitter users is split pretty evenly over every age demographic. In fact, the fastest growing demographic on

Facebook is 55- to 65-year-old women. Why? Because grandma is signing up to look at photos of little Johnny and then realizing that all of her friends and family are actively engaged and … that's FUN!

6. "Status updates on Facebook and tweets on Twitter are stupid. Who cares about what everyone is doing all the time?"

Many artists are wary of Twitter and Facebook updates because they don't feel that people want to know their random or personal thoughts. And they don't want to "waste their time" using them.

Also, many artists feel that social networking sites are made for promotional use (only). When we all came to the party with the first ever social network (the now all-but-dead Myspace), that was indeed the case. In fact the *goal* on Myspace was: hype, hype, hype, promote, and add, add, add as many friends as possible. Rack up the plays by any means necessary, or you wouldn't get that club booker to pay, give you the gig, or get that record label to sign you! There were very few personal thoughts or "status updates" in the Myspace mix.

Twitter and Facebook are community-building and sharing platforms as opposed to promotional tools, so it confuses artists when it comes to what they are supposed to be contributing.

7. "I don't want my fans to see my personal life."

The empowering thing about social media is you can show only what you want to show; not everything is so personal. Here are a few ideas to start with: movies you like, books you read, and other artists you love and respect, and why.

D. TRADITIONAL MEDIA VS. SOCIAL MEDIA

The key differentiator between traditional and social media is YOU

Social media consists of platforms that most likely make you uncomfortable. However, if your goal is to capture and maintain an audience, social media is the only free and fully-populated platform able to get you there.

The amazing thing about social media is: if the mainstream print media "rejects" you, or if you can't afford access, you now have more power than ever before to take matters into your own hands and connect directly.

As traditional media outlets and formats (such as newspapers) continue their decline, social networks have become integral platforms for engaging fans and consumers who, according to surveys, are expecting to be engaged more and more as time rolls on.

Traditional media works like this: You get reviewed in a newspaper or magazine, or get interviewed on radio or TV. It's broadcast out into the world. People read the magazine or newspaper, watch TV or listen in. Traditional media operates like a ONE-WAY street, passively delivering content to viewers and listeners.

Social media is completely different. It's a TWO-WAY, interactive street. You are not only invited to participate, but also encouraged to do so. Platforms like Facebook, Twitter and blogs facilitate easy and transparent participation, and all who are connected can see, react, and participate with your social media posts and activity.

If you are used to the "traditional model," this TWO-WAY street is foreign, unfamiliar, overwhelming and not what you signed up for when you decided you wanted to share your vision with the world.

For those still in that mindset, I have three words: **adapt or die**.

E. THE MAIN FEATURES OF WEB 2.0

Web 1.0 is the Internet we all grew up on, where websites were simply pages of information for you to read. Most business websites were nothing more than an online brochure that included the same kind of information: Home Page, About, Bio, Mission, Buy, Contact Us, etc. You may still have one of these websites right now.

In the days of Web 1.0, you "surfed the net" to check out websites and found information, which was always presented to you as a one-way conversation — something to read (or click away from).

Web 2.0 allows you to interact and collaborate with others and create new content, as opposed to simply viewing content. It's all about the two-way conversation and interacting, engaging, and connecting. In other words, it's social rather than static! And it requires participation.

As an artist with a presence in the Web 2.0 landscape, you can connect on a more personal level with social media makers and fans. By creating strong social networking profiles, keeping them fed with great content and by practicing engagement, you are much more visible online. You also have many more opportunities through which potential fans can learn about you.

SUCCESSFUL MEDIA PRESENCE DOESN'T HAPPEN OVERNIGHT

Each social media site has its own protocols, as well as its own mood and emphasis. As you get to know each one and build a following, you'll start to reap the benefits of engaging within each community.

My suggestion is: dig in and get comfortable with one social media platform before you join or master a second, then a third, etc. Eventually, you will want to join and engage on multiple networks. Doing so gives you more exposure and more opportunities to attract fans and make money.

TENDING TO YOUR SOCIAL MEDIA HOUSE

Web 2.0 is like a house. If you have owned a house, you know that you can't just buy a house and ignore it. A house needs constant attention and upkeep; everything from doing home repairs to weeding your garden. Neglecting your Social Media House, by leaving static pages on social media, is not the way to keep it up properly.

MAKING IT IN MUSIC IS HARD

Making it in music is hard, no matter what side of the fence you are on. My friends who are managers, agents, and club owners work just as hard as my artist friends. Record label employees are still getting laid off left and right. This game that we all choose to play is not for the meek!

And now you, as the artist, are required to do a *whole lot more* than you might have had to even just a few years ago. Just remember:

1. The basic rules for success are still the same.

2. In order to increase your bottom line, you *must* focus on your fans!

F. UNDERSTANDING THE RULES OF ENGAGEMENT

I once attended a life-changing workshop called the "World's Greatest Marketing Seminar," which was designed to help entrepreneurs with marketing. One of the most successful entrepreneur speakers stood up on stage and delivered some horrible news:

"In order to be successful, 70 percent of your time should be spent on your marketing and sales, and 30 percent working on your business."

There was a collective gasp in the audience.

This will apply to you, too, because every successful artist also has to market effectively. Yes, this means that as artists you still must balance the creation of your art, but you better spend a lot more time on the marketing side, (much more time than you probably thought you needed to).

HOW DO YOU DO THIS?

Watch the amazing 14-minute TED talk where Amanda Palmer tells you how the first step towards obtaining fans is building rapport with everyone you come in contact with, not only in person, but also using social media and your email list. See the video here: http://bit.ly/AmandaTED

Everyone always references the astonishing Amanda Palmer as the poster child for success with this kind of relationship. As I write this book, Amanda has just broken every single indie artist record in the book for fan funding by raising over $1 million from her fans. It's incredible and totally awe-inspiring. How did she do it?

AMANDA PALMER REALLY FOCUSES ON HER FANS

Amanda STAYS at the venue after each and every show, signing every CD, piece of merch and scrap of paper put in front of her.

She STAYS until she has personally touched the last fan waiting.

Then, she STAYS in touch with them long after she has left their town with her newsletter, her blog, her Facebook posts and her Twitter stream. Amanda Palmer understands the rules of engagement. It's not magic—it's hard work. And what may amaze and hopefully inspire you is that she genuinely loves the connections that she has fostered.

You may not have the large number of fans Amanda has to get to a million dollars (yet), but you can have what she has too, and here are three very important basics that can help get you there.

G. NO HOUSE CAN STAND WITHOUT A FOUNDATION

THREE VERY IMPORTANT BASICS

Before I dive in and focus on Facebook, Twitter, YouTube and all other social media sites that drive you bonkers, we are going to start with three very important basics. This foundation will give you a context as you dive in and master the technical aspects of social media and online presence in this book. Just grasping these three broad strokes will help you instantly. They are: 1. Your Newsletter List, 2. Your Product Line, and 3. Fan Feedback.

1. Your Newsletter

I have seen it countless times – artists misuse their email lists by only reaching out to their fans when they have something to sell them (a show, a new release etc.) but they never reach out to their fans for other reasons: to bond, share a funny story, or invite everyone out to the local bowling alley on a Tuesday night for a hang.

Every study on sales has proven one thing: Most people resist when they feel they are being "sold to" (think of the typical used car salesman archetype we all dislike), however, people love to buy, and people always love to buy from people whom they like and trust. People in Amanda Palmers' circle of followers trust her.

Great salespeople sell by creating relationships with their customers, and are able to stay in their customer's hearts and minds until the customer is ready to buy.

Now, you may be freaking out here a bit. In your head, your *fans* are not *customers*. You don't want to consider fans in this light. I understand this, but I am asking you to shift from your artist mind for a moment and get into your business head.

Your fans are *indeed* your customers. They give you money to support your creative livelihood. There are two things to ask yourself here based on looking at it in this light:

a. Do you have a fan base to sell to?

This means:

- An email list

- An active Facebook community

- Twitter followers

- Blog readers

If not, don't worry. This book will teach you how to do all this and more.

b. How big is your fan base?

I consider a real fan base a minimum of 5,000 people across your social networks and 1,000 on your email list. Once you have a large enough fan base to ask, you can begin to make money when you engage wisely.

2. Your Product Line

If you only sell CDs and MP3s then you do not have a product line. Along this journey I will make many suggestions for possible assorted merchandise and offerings.

Some ideas include:

- A fan club

- Monthly offerings

- Private events (parties, weddings or BBQs)

- Merch your fans may want (coffee mugs or yoga mats)

3. Fan Feedback (AKA Your Survey Strategy)

Have you ever asked your fans what they might want to buy? Amanda Palmer knew EXACTLY what to offer in her groundbreaking Kickstarter campaign because she was consistently talking to her fans, so it was no surprise when they started buying everything she sold with gusto! Pull in all of your talents. Do you paint? Do you write? Do you bake?

If you ever decide to launch a fan funding campaign you may want to tie in your additional talents while you raise money allowing your fans to support you even more!

That's how Amanda got to a million bucks; she leveraged all of her artist friends (over 30 of them all together) to join in and made the offer even sweeter for her fans.

H. ARIEL'S SOUND TAKEAWAYS

- Social media is here to stay—ignoring it will make you obsolete. It's time to grab the bull by the horns.

- You first must enjoy the journey and embrace it. If you don't really like connecting with people and you don't care, social media may not be for you, and you should reconsider this as a strategy (watch Amanda Palmer's TED talk video to see an artist in action embracing this)

- People of all ages, races, and economic demographics use social media. That means that you can and will find your tribe—it's just now a matter of learning how.

- Social media puts you in control and in the driver's seat. That is a deeply powerful place to be, because from here you can map out your own journey.

- Begin to identify your niches—they are your keys.

- Newsletter, product line, and fan feedback will be augmented and solidified with proper social media use.

- Create products to satisfy your fans!

- Build your email list! Every day think about whom you can get on your list.

- When your list gets to be at least 1,000 strong, *ask* your fans what they may like from you and how much they will pay.

CHAPTER 1: *Website*

A. THE FRONT DOOR OF YOUR SOCIAL MEDIA HOUSE

The next several chapters in this book are dedicated to the five rooms that make up your Social Media House. We will go through each one carefully, and then, at the end of the book, we will talk about devising a real plan for getting the Social Media House into practice for a real or sample client.

This is the front door of your Social Media House. Come on in and wipe your shoes at the door!

YOUR WEBSITE IS YOUR FRONT DOOR

You can't enter a house without a front door.

Keeping up with all of the developments and strategies in the online space can be a tough job. As soon as you master a social platform or technique that works, it may change (hello, Facebook). One thing that doesn't change and never will is this: Your entire online presence starts at your website. Social media is where a lot of action and conversation takes place but your website is the part of your online house that you built and own. Social sites may come and go, but your website is yours (as long as you pay your hosting fees!). This is why it is crucial to keep your website updated.

B. NICHES ARE THE KEYS TO YOUR SOCIAL MEDIA HOUSE

Before I dive in and overwhelm you with the foundation, the front door, and all of the rooms of the Social Media House, I want you to take this into careful consideration: the Internet is a huge wide open place full of countless opportunities. The more focused you are the easier it will be to connect and build your audience swiftly. The golden keys that unlock the door are your niches.

Here's what it comes down to. If a niche exists, so does a network of bloggers who are passionate about it. (Remember, there are more than 200 million bloggers!)

A FEW EXAMPLE BLOG NICHES TO CONSIDER

Humanitarian	Travel	Yoga
Charity/Causes	Cancer/Survival	Teen/Tween
Pets/Animal Rescue	Politics	Cooking/Recipes
Religion	Positivity	Eco/Green
Your Community	Your City/State	Health
Gardening	Crafting	Books/Reading
Vegan/Gluten-Free	Fashion	Parenting

Yes, I know - the first thing you will (hopefully) notice is that none of these niches have a single thing to do with music. I've seen it time and time again, smaller artists go gunning for the largest websites they can find and are mystified and disappointed when they don't get their music reviewed and covered on coveted blogs such as pitchfork.com.

With 2,000 new releases every single week and hipster, indie rock music blogs taking up the lion's share of "music writing" these days, your options are limited if you do not fall into a specific niche.

Before you dive into the rest of this book I strongly recommend that you write down five distinct niches that will set you apart from the rest and have nothing to do with musical genres. This can change over time. Dog-ear this page, and write in pencil if you want to come back and change these later.

1. _____

2. _____

3. _____

4. _____

5. _____

C. THE CYBER PR® GUIDE TO AFFORDABLE, EFFECTIVE WEBSITES

One of the biggest myths about having an effective online presence is that you need to pay a lot of money for a website.

Back in 1997, when we all started thinking about getting a web presence it was normal to meet Web designers who wanted to charge five or ten thousand dollars to build you a website. It's not 1997 anymore, and prices like that are relics in the past.

An effective website can now be created for $20 or less a month with no upfront costs. So for those of you who need a template and an idea of how to get started on an affordable website (and how to design it), this guide is for you.

Many artists make themselves crazy when building websites because they have trouble keeping it simple, and this is the key. Your website exists to do two things:

1. Help you engage with, and make new fans.
2. Make you money.

RESPONSIVE DESIGN

A new paradigm for web design has taken over. It's known as responsive design. In essence, responsive design means the user will have one universal experience—content is delivered the same way no matter what device it's viewed on. With the growth of portable devices like smartphones and tablets, this is crucial to consider.

Back in the day, web designers created websites designed exclusively for laptop or desktop users. They would pull their hair out to create a site design that looked good on, let's say a Blackberry, but the site would end up looking horrible on a laptop, and vice versa.

Responsive design makes much more sense. It means that your website & branding will be delivered to your audience and fans without worrying whether it was viewed properly.

Using universal programming standards recently accepted by all the major mobile device companies; responsive website designs have become streamlined and efficient. Designers are even adding now-commonplace swiping and pinching hand gestures. In a playing field full of competition for eyeballs, you want your potential fans to be hooked into your content within the first 3.5 seconds, not to be frustrated by bad design that fails to introduce your content properly.

Don't get too worried by the term "Responsive Design." Even Hostbaby's templates now offer it—it doesn't cost extra money, and it's not more difficult to design—you just want to make sure you ask for it if you are redesigning your site or starting from scratch.

HOW TO SET YOURSELF ON THE RIGHT PATH:

STEP 1: You must have a domain name. To register a domain name go somewhere like godaddy.com (USA) or crazydomains.com.au (AUS).

Register the domain that you would like to use. I highly suggest a dot com (.com) if you can get one, with no dashes, dots, or underscores.

TIP: You should make sure that the corresponding YouTube, Twitter and Facebook page names are also available. It is important to make sure your social media sites match.

STEP 2: Choose which option you would like (a. Free, b. Pay-as-You-Go, or c. Work with a Web Designer).

a. Free!

A free site owned by AOL called About.me is one of the best ways to start your first footprints on the web. Using widely accepted search optimization formatting, it allows you to build and design your own webpage attached to your own choice of URL.

My page on about.me

You can enter as much information as you wish, but the real benefit is that you can feed in all your social streams, upload a photo and personalize your page to fit the direction of your brand. About.me also supplies you with your own email inbox, and you can connect with www.moo.com cards to create your own free About.me business cards. The site also has widely available smartphone and tablet apps so you can easily update your page.

b. Pay-as-You-Go

A pay-as-you-go option with a website builder can get you up and running very quickly and you won't need a designer to build for you. Here are my favorite four sites that host musician and band websites. All have excellent call-in customer service to help ease the confusion. All also have tons of fabulous templates to choose from and many social media options and plug-ins to bring social media into your site layout.

Bandzoogle - http://bandzoogle.com

Bombplates - http://www.bombplates.com

Hostbaby - http://www.hostbaby.com

Nimbit - http://www.nimbit.com

An example of a site designed with HostBaby.

c. Working With a Web Designer

Wordpress - http://wordpress.com

Don't pay more than $500 for a basic WordPress site.

I suggest http://www.crowdspring.com or http://www.linkedin.com for finding affordable WordPress designers. Make sure you read the designer's reviews and see examples of his or her work before you hire him or her so you don't get any unpleasant surprises.

Don't work with an "artsy" Web designer who does not build in WordPress because he or she will give you a Flash movie intro or some kind of complicated site. If you want artsy, buy a fabulous new outfit, or create a physical piece of merchandise that's really cool, and expresses who you are. But please don't be "artsy" on your website.

GoSpacecraft - http://gospacecraft.com

GoSpacecraft is a growing responsive website design service. For the cost of about $500-600 per year, they do the initial startup design for you, as well as any updates. Similar to Wordpress, GoSpacecraft works via a custom interface, where you have control of posting, editing and updating all content. They use their own cloud based web hosting, that is fueled by unlimited bandwidth. You get monthly or yearly payment options, with included tech support. Adding the standard social media plug in's is as simple as a few mouse clicks. Overall, its one of the cleanest responsive design platforms out there. There's a 14-day free trial so you can test it out to see if you like it before committing.

NINE STEPS TO A GREAT HOME PAGE

1. Your entire website should be easy to navigate with a nav. bar across the very top of each page or down the left hand side (at the top) so visitors can see it, (not buried where they have to scroll down).

2. Create a unified brand with your look, your colors, and your logo (if you have a logo) and of course a stunning photo of you/your band.

TIP: Your social media sites should all match your site colors.

An example of a well-designed, effective home page using Bandzoogle.

3. Your social media sites should feature your name and your pitch (or specifically what you sound like in a few words). If you feel weird creating a "pitch," use one killer press quote or fan quote that sums up the way you sound.

4. Feature a free MP3 in exchange for an email address.

TIP: Use ReverbNation, PledgeMusic, Topspin, and NoiseTrade widgets.

> **ReverbNation** - http://www.bit.ly/reverbfreebribe
>
> **PledgeMusic** - http://www.bit.ly/pledgefreebribe
>
> **NoiseTrade** - http://www.noisetrade.com
>
> **TopSpin** - http://www.topspinmedia.com

5. Link your home page to your social media: Facebook, Twitter, YouTube, Pinterest, ReverbNation, Sonicbids, Last.fm, and anywhere else you maintain an active profile.

6. Include a Facebook "like" widget.

7. Include a Twitter stream or a group Tweet stream (updating in real time).

8. A blog feed/news feed, or new shows updating onto the page via widgets.

9. If you like sharing photos, use a Flickr or Instagram stream, which imports over to your blog!

NAVIGATION BAR ELEMENTS AND TABS

It is crucial to think through how you present yourself to people who may want to write about you, feature you, or share your music. More and more we see online tastemakers influencing their friends; having elements and assets that are easy for visitors to grab and share will make this a win-win for you both.

1. Bio/Press Kit. For Your Press Kits use Sonicbids or ReverbNation.

TIP: Photos/Images. Make sure your photos really capture who you are. Make sure they have clear instructions on how they can be downloaded.

2. Buy Music – iTunes or a Storefront

3. Your Tour Shows or Live Performances

4. Your Blog: Link to Tumblr, Wordpress or Blogger

5. Your Contact Info

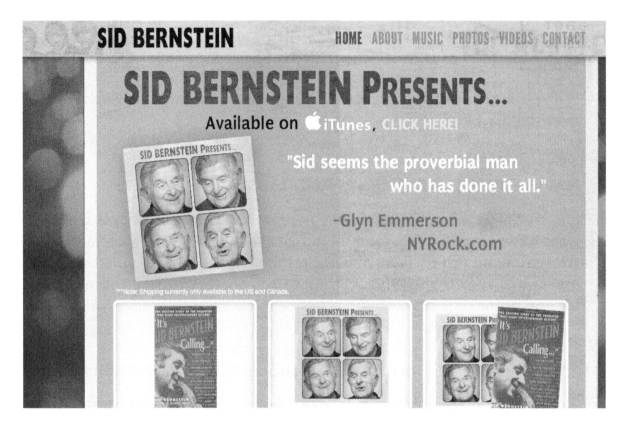

Great example of simple, effective navigation

Don't make it hard for anyone to find you online. Make sure you have your contact information with an email address or a contact form here so people can contact you for online publicity, booking, or just to tell you they like your music.

After your site is done, make sure to keep your social media sites updated! (That means daily.) This way, your site remains interesting and current.

The front door of your Social Media House is now complete. Your biggest fans will be the first ones through that door (to your website).

Before we dive into the various rooms that will comprise your house, I want to discuss the fans that will be coming to your social media sites and how to think about marketing to them. The main objective is you want to funnel all fans to your front door and to your mailing list.

NAVIGATION BAR ELEMENTS AND TABS

I am amazed how hard it can be to find simple press components on many artists' websites. Here are 3 critical components that you should include on the press page of your website. These components show music writers and calendar editors that you care about making their lives easier. Editors need access to your information quickly, because they are constantly under a deadline. If you do not make it easy for them to get your information from your site, they may move onto another one of the 50 artists that are playing their market that same week.

1. Your Music—Album or Live Tracks

Make sure you have some music available on your website or a very obvious link to your Facebook where people can hear the music instantly. Many newspapers are now including MP3s of artists coming to town in the online versions of their papers, so make it easy for them to download the tracks to add to their own sites; this is additional excellent exposure for you.

2. Biography—Must Include Your Pitch

Make sure you have a short, succinct bio that can be easily located on your site in addition to the long-form bio. I suggest having three bios:

   1. Long form

   2. 50 words or less

   3. 130 characters (a tweet plus a username)

Make sure this bio can be easily cut and pasted so writers can drop it into a preview or a column. Also include a short summary (less than 10 words)—your pitch—that sums up your sound for calendar editors.

You can also include the blogs and all the opinions from each band member. But remember that while these extras are fun for your fans, they are not necessarily useful for music writers who will be looking to get quick information.

TIP: Do NOT have your bio in Flash format, so cutting and pasting right off your site is easy for editors.

3. Photos—Make Them Easy to Find and Download

Thumbnails are great for quick and easy loading, but are detrimental for use in newspapers. You should always have a few downloadable photos on your site in at least 300 dpi/jpg format.

TIP #1: Create an easy-to-see link that says "click here for a hi-res jpg." That way photo editors can get to them easily. When the photos are downloaded, make sure they are properly named with your name or your band's name, so that photo editors can find them in folders.

TIP #2: Remember to change your photos a few times a year, so if you play the same markets over and over, you can give the media multiple options for covering you.

TIP #3: Put the band members' names from left to right (L-R) under the band photo to give journalists a point of reference. Many publications publish photos with all band members' names from left to right to save the writers the trouble of having to ask for the names.

4. Include Your Album Cover Artwork

You also want to make sure you include your cover art in both hi-res and lo-res (jpg) format. This way if your CD is being reviewed, the writer can download the artwork.

D. YOUR THREE COMMUNITIES

Now that you have a website, and have entered the door to your Social Media House, what is your goal? You may be getting tripped up because you do not see the big picture or fully understand the real reason why all of these seemingly stupid and mundane online tasks are relevant. So, I have parsed the fans into three communities to give you some context. Your audience is not just one, lumped-together, group of people; it is, in fact, three very separate communities and you need to think about how you approach each of these communities differently.

COMMUNITY #1: Super Fans

COMMUNITY #2: Engaged Fans

COMMUNITY #3: Ambient Fans

COMMUNITY #1: SUPER FANS

Your Super Fans are primarily your live audience members. You know them by name. If you play out, they attend your shows regularly, and buy many things you have to offer (not just your music). If you have a street team, they are on it and they evangelize strongly on your behalf.

Your live audience (if you play out) and your "real" friends who support you are included in this group. They will most likely be the first engaged community you have and the first one you started building.

Much has changed in the past few years. Before social media was around, their group of Super Fans was the only community that independent musicians really had. Back before social media, you fostered relationships with Community #1 by playing live often and you captivated them in person.

You didn't need to grab them within the first few seconds online because they most likely stuck around for at least a few songs. You didn't have to worry about a "15 second pitch" (or elevator pitch) to describe what you sounded like because you were up on stage for them to see. And you didn't have to worry about the load time on your website, and all of your social media chops. You just had to BRING IT playing live ... Then you could build your mailing list and your fan base in person.

In other words, back in the day, if you could rope in potential fans by playing a compelling live show, you were on your way to having a true fan base of engaged fans. That still holds true today.

HOW TO ENGAGE SUPER FANS

1. Make Great Music: This always comes up when you ask the experts – making great music is (and has to be) the foundation. Always be honing your craft and working to make sure your music is the best it can be.

2. Create a Riveting Live Show: When you create an incredible live show, you will be (in the words of expert marketer Seth Godin) "remarkable."

> "Remarkable doesn't mean remarkable to you. It means remarkable to me. Am I going to make a remark about it? If not, then you're average, and average is for losers."
>
> - Seth Godin

3. Consider all of the following bullet points:

- Connection to the audience
- A fantastic live show
- The audience's experience
- Solid songwriting
- Great music
- Word of mouth

IMPROVING YOUR SHOW

Tom Jackson is the most extraordinary live music coach I've ever watched in action. Tom works on developing his clients' live stage shows using a series of effective techniques to both create a cohesive show and a connection with the live audience.

Tom rightly points out that your songs don't all sound the same, but in most cases when you perform live, they all look the same. Tom's DVDs, blog and workshops will help you work on your solo performance, band dynamic, and stage presence. I have seen him work miracles with musicians. In just a few hours, he completely transforms shows that are humdrum into riveting stage performances. Tom is unlike any coach out there, and what he teaches needs to be seen in order to be fully understood.

See what he does here: http://bit.ly/TomJacksonCoach

CAPTURING DATA FROM SUPER FANS

Once the live audience is at your gig, ask them for their email addresses so they can receive your newsletter, or for their mobile numbers so you can add them to your text messaging list. You should employ consistent techniques to communicate with them. Also, add a column to your newsletter sign up sheet asking fans, "Is it okay if we find you on Facebook? Y/N." And lastly, add a Twitter column so they can write their Twitter handles (usernames).

If you have not made a concerted effort to connect the dots between your live audience and your email list, you are sacrificing a direct line to money. Sign up for a newsletter management system to help get you on the way. We recommend ReverbNation, Bandletter, Fanbridge, or Nimbit to get started. More on that is coming later in this book, fear not!

COMMUNITY #2: ENGAGED FANS

Engaged Fans are your active online audience, but not the people who show up at every gig. They are newsletter subscribers, blog readers, video watchers, RSS subscribers, active social media engagers who frequently comment and engage with you on Facebook, Twitter, and other sites you use. In Community #2, contribution is critical, but engagement is even more vital. In order to create engagement, you need to give Community #2 something to be engaged with. The secret here is creating content.

Brian Solis, the author of two of my favorite books about PR and social media, "Engage" and the co-author of "Putting the Public Back in Public Relations" wrote a brilliant blog post on the reasons why creating content is a necessity in today's social media landscape: Content speaks DIRECTLY to your already-engaged fans and draws them in deeper.

The title of his blog post is "The Future of Marketing Starts with Publishing." It's written for businesses. Music is your business, so it won't take much reading between the lines to decipher a plan for yourself.

Here are the two most amazing morsels from the post:

> "Creating social profiles and broadcasting tweets and status updates is elementary, whereas creating a meaningful presence through the development and dissemination of remarkable content is judicious ...

> " ... Time and attention are precious commodities and therefore require thoughtful commentary, involvement, contribution, and programming to spark actions and reactions and concurrently earn two-way alliances that ultimately form the relationships businesses need to cultivate communities and also inspire advocacy."

> - Brian Solis

So now that you see why creating content on a regular basis is key, here are my tips for engaging Community #2 as you go along:

FIVE TIPS FOR ENGAGING AND INSPIRING ENGAGED FANS

1. Create A Monthly Newsletter – With ONE Call To Action (CTA)

Examples of Calls to Action are:

- Join my Facebook Fan Page

- Follow Me On Twitter

- Subscribe to my RSS / blog feed

If you don't have a newsletter, you are ripping yourself off! Start sending one now (even if its only to 25 people to start). Only have one Call To Action per monthly communication – too many will confuse people. If you are a bit lost on how to create a newsletter, fear not! That will be coming later in this book.

2. Add a Social Media Column to Your Newsletter Signup Sheets

When at gigs or creating an online signup form: Don't just ask for their email; ask for their Twitter and Facebook pages as well!

How? Easy: Simply add a column that says: "Is it okay if I find you on Facebook, Twitter, etc.? If so please enter your @[TwitterName] and Facebook username.

3. Use Derek Sivers' Ultimate Fan Engagement Tip

Take photos or videos at every single show from the stage (these will be focusing on the audience) and at the merch table of the fans who come up to talk to you and/or purchase merchandise ("merch") from you. Create a separate photo album for each show on Facebook, Pinterest, Instagram, or Flickr. Link these to your blog and to your Facebook status updates. As you add everyone to the mailing list, point them to each photo set featuring: Them! They will be very likely to go check themselves out, and the best part is – they will share those photos with their friends too.

TIP: People are more interested in themselves than they are in you. Make them the main attraction. These fans will also be delighted that they have been included.

4. Create Checklists for Systematizing the Building of Your Online Presence

With all of the social media platforms you need to keep up with, it can be easy to miss vital opportunities where people can run into you. So, create a show checklist for every time you confirmed a show, go through it and systematically check off each action you need to take, you would never miss a beat in your online live music promotion. Some examples of what you may want to add to your checklist are:

- Create an event on Facebook: Invite appropriate friends based on location by using lists or groups

- Update ReverbNation/Artistdata/BandsinTown widget: It will add the show to Facebook, Twitter, blog, and on your website

- Blog about the upcoming event: Cross-post to all sites

- Tweet the event using a bit.ly link

- Remember to share engaging updates about what you are doing, and that it is just as important as contributing because it shows a more human side of you

- Sell tickets and additional merch on Facebook using Nimbit.com or the fabulous CD Baby Facebook app

- Create a photo album in Facebook and a Pinterest board for each city you play in (if you don't play out create one for all the cities you love and visit)

- It's about leading them back to your website—always keep this in mind!

5. Parse Your Friends Into Geographical Lists and Facebook Groups

Another great tactic is parsing out your fans so they are grouped geographically by where people live. You will see 95 percent of musicians don't know how to do this and their messages are being ignored on Facebook.

A proper newsletter service will allow you to create sub groups which you can parse geographically by city/town you tour in.

If your Facebook friends have said where they live on their pages, you can do a search by location then you can personalize each show message so you won't be spamming people who live in Duluth for a show in Los Angeles.

COMMUNITY #3: AMBIENT FANS

The New York Times Magazine ran an article written by Clive Thompson, called "Brave New World of Digital Intimacy" that redefined how people think and brilliantly talked about how social scientists refer to how we connect to one another using social media as "ambient awareness."

It's described like this:

> "[Ambient awareness is] very much like being physically near someone and picking up on his mood through the little things he does — body language, sighs, stray comments — out of the corner of your eye. Facebook is no longer alone in offering this sort of interaction online. In the last year, there has been a boom in tools for "micro-blogging": posting frequent tiny updates on what you're doing. The phenomenon is quite different from what we normally think of as blogging, because a blog post is usually a written piece, sometimes quite long: a statement of opinion, a story, an analysis. But these new updates are something different. They're far shorter, far more frequent and less carefully considered. One of the most popular new tools is Twitter."

> - Clive Thompson

Ambient Fans are your Passive Online Audience and they are your social media friends who are aware of you via Twitter, Facebook, YouTube, Pinterest etc., but don't actively communicate with you, and may not have heard your music (yet).

According to Thompson (and I concur), people do care about the things you think they don't care about, like your tuna sandwich. Here's why (and this is my favorite part of the article):

> "Each little update — each individual bit of social information — is insignificant on its own, even supremely mundane. But taken together, over time, the little snippets coalesce into a surprisingly sophisticated portrait of your friends' and family members' lives…This was never before possible, because in the real world, no friend would bother to call you up and detail the sandwiches she was eating."
>
> - Clive Thompson

The key to converting Community #3 members into Community #2 members, or ambient into engaged fans, is sharing relevant information mixed in with the simple and seemly mundane.

I was once chatting with a dear friend about social media and she confided in me about her distaste for mundane updates, I hate all these people who just update stupid things like 'I'm drinking coffee' – I mean who cares?" I started smirking because I have written just such a coffee tweet on many occasions.

"I tweet about my coffee all of the time," I pointed out to her.

She paused, "Yes, but you also tweet interesting articles and blog posts about the music business, updates on cool places to eat, shop, and visit as well as I get to pretend I'm with you having that coffee when you travel."

Granted, she's already in my Community #1. Therefore, I am relevant to her. My coffee tweets don't bother her in the least, but I bet if I never shared other things she found relevant, she would pay no attention to me at all.

So, you may be asking: What constitutes as relevant?

The simple answer is, if it is relevant to you, it's probably relevant to your three Communities.

TIP: IMPORTANT! On Facebook and Twitter, you first must follow people back who follow you. It's the polite thing to do because it says I am equally as interested in you as you are in me! This is the cornerstone.

HOW TO ENGAGE AMBIENT FANS

Artist objection: Do I HAVE to follow these people? I don't care about them.

My answer: YES. If you don't care about potential fans and getting into a relationship with you, then they should not care about you.

Artist objection: But I can't manage looking at thousands of updates - I will miss the ones I care about...

My answer: I understand. But in this world of two-way communication, you need to think about those relationships. Social media is here to stay. Luckily, there are some fabulous applications for managing and screening out the good stuff from the river of overwhelm.

MOVIE TIME!

To watch Ariel give a full presentation about the three communities in action watch this video. This is a keynote she delivered at MIDEM, illustrating how to move fans from Community #1 to Community #3.

Three Distribution Loop: http://bit.ly/DistroLoopMIDEM

E. CYBER PR®'s SOCIAL MEDIA PYRAMID

FOOD PYRAMID

I've been told they don't actually teach this in school anymore… but for those of you old enough to remember, do you recall the chart they brought out when we were in second grade to show us how to eat well-rounded meals? I have re-tooled it for you so you can now participate in social media in a healthy, well-rounded way! And you won't even have to think about it – just follow along. (The inspiration for this hit me while I was teaching my system to a client in my kitchen.)

You probably shouldn't eat only bagels all of the time. They are a treat once in a while, but they are not healthy to eat every day, and besides that, a diet of only bagels would be boring!

If we take that metaphor to music publicity, most artists are only serving their audiences bagels all the time. Plain bagels. Over and over again. Uninteresting!

We want a burger, or a giant green healthy salad, we want some candy. We want protein, but you keep serving bagels, bagels, bagels!

The Social Media Pyramid has five kinds of activity that you can use in concert, in order to ratchet up your social media effectively and manage it easily. Feel free to mix and match within these activities in order to suit your comfort level.

SOCIAL MEDIA PYRAMID

When I'm teaching artists about social media, the following scenario plays out just about all the time. Their face goes pale, the frustration begins to settle in, and then the artist says what I'm waiting to hear: "I just don't have anything interesting to say."

REALLY? I'm shocked by this every time. You are an *artist*; you do things we mere *mortals* are totally enamored by: you PLAY MUSIC, you write songs, you perform them in public! So PUH-*LEEASE*, do not tell me you have nothing interesting to say. I ain't buying it.

All you are missing is a system for your social media success. Luckily, unlike sheer God-given musical talent, social media is a learnable skill.

The following sections explain the Social Media Pyramid in a narrative format. The two-page diagram follows.

GROUP ONE: DIRECT ENGAGEMENT

Similar to: BREAD, CEREAL, RICE & PASTA
Servings (Recommended Frequency): 3-4 out of every 10 posts

Make sure you're in a two-way conversation with people consistently.

 Facebook

See something interesting on a fan, friend, or band's Facebook pages? Don't just "like" it, write a true comment about it and get more involved.

 Twitter

Send messages to people or mention you are with them by using the @ sign and their username (For Example: I'm @CyberPR). Retweet (RT) comments you like by others.

 Blog Reading

Create a Google Profile and join communities of blog readers. Leave comments on blogs you like. Google Profiles are now attached to your Google+ account so make sure to set up your Google+ account as well!

 Tumblr

Tumblr is a simple to use blogging platform that will allow you to comment on and re-blog others' links, quotes, videos and songs with the click of a button.

 YouTube

Make custom video comments or greetings with a smartphone; post them as comments or contributions. Subscribe to other people's channels, and comment on their videos.

Foursquare

Create fun spots that relate to your band/music and check in, interact with others when you are out and about. Of course, Facebook now has Facebook Places which functions quite similarly, though it doesn't have nearly as much functionality in terms of making lists and engaging as its own stand alone platform.

GROUP TWO: SHINE A LIGHT ON OTHERS

Similar to: FRUITS & VEGETABLES
Servings (Recommended Frequency): 3 out of every 10 posts

All the best social media users know this and use it well. This takes all of the attention off you and puts it onto others. People will appreciate your kindness because you are recognizing them in front of new potential fans and followers, therefore helping them get known.

Quote people you like by sharing their profiles and videos on Facebook and re-post on your blog. Link to articles and interesting things that catch your attention such as videos, photos etc.

#FF (Follow Friday), #MM (Music Monday) and RTing on Twitter - Reprint pieces of things you like, or link to music players. Review albums – talk about why and how those albums influenced you by using http://bit.ly to track effectiveness and to shorten your tweets.

GROUP THREE: CURATE CONTENT

Similar to: MEAT, POULTRY, FISH, BEANS, EGGS
Servings (Recommended Frequency): 2 – 3 out of every 10 posts

Content may be king, but content curation is queen!

The best part is you can set up an RSS reader to pull interesting content for you so you don't have to come up with anything brilliant – just select what you like and share it. If it's interesting to you, it's probably interesting to your community.

Ask yourself: How do I spend time online? What do I read? Are there sites I visit daily? Add them to the RSS reader (here is a brilliant Commoncraft video that will teach you how to set one up. Then all you have to do is grab the content you like and share (remember to always give credit where credit is due). http://www.commoncraft.com/video/rss

- Music: Use Spotify and/or Rdio to share songs, albums and playlists on Facebook.

- Recipes: Post links to foods you like from Epicurious or The Food Network

- Media: Post book reviews, music reviews or film reviews

- Blogs: News, politics, celebrity gossip, parenting, fashion, art, sports – all make good topics for people to connect around

GROUP FOUR: A PICTURE SAYS 1,000 WORDS

Similar to: MILK, CHEESE & YOGURT
Servings (Recommended Frequency): 2 out of every 10 posts

Visuals are extremely effective. And they mix up your strategy nicely.

Take photos using your mobile and post them to Facebook and Twitter. If you have an iPhone, the best way to do this is with the Instagram app.

I love Twitpic and YFrog because they are so easy to use and create instant Twitter integration.

Pinterest is a wonderful way to share photos of anything you are passionate about, and create some boards for your music and merch too.

Post videos on your custom YouTube channel, embed them on your blog and link them to your Twitter. They don't even have to be videos that you necessarily make on your own. They can be videos of artists you sound like or play with, videos that make you laugh, or subjects that are thematic to your music and important to you, like a charity.

GROUP FIVE: SHINING A LIGHT ON YOURSELF (SELF-PROMOTION)

Like: FATS, OILS & SWEETS (Use Sparingly!)
Servings (Recommended Frequency): 1 out of every 10 posts

Of course these are okay to do once in a while, not in an over-hype-y, annoying way. Just like treating yourself to a great pastry or some fries: its okay – but not too often!

It is after all, vital to tell people if you have an album coming out, a new track, a show, or anything that's newsworthy or noteworthy for your fans and followers to know about.

Don't forget about your specific calls to action or these won't be fruitful.

So – Choose from Groups 1-5 and mix it up and soon you will be fully engaging people easily and naturally, without thinking. Just like eating!

F. ARIEL'S SOUND TAKEAWAYS

- It is important that you identify your niches before you take on re-building or creating your website go to the niches exercise before you build, edit or rebrand - this will focus you to think in new ways

- Assess what you need to do for your site, whether a touch-up or full rebuild

- Which plan will you choose?
  a. Free
  b. Pay as you go
  c. Work with a designer

- Make sure your site is easily updatable by you (and you are not beholden to anyone but you!)

- Create a personalized system for site updates that you can follow so you have a system

- Create step-by-step systems so that your team or interns can follow as well!

- Understand The Three Communities and begin to mentally assess which fans fit where when you make contact with them

- Post the Social Media Pyramid in your studio to keep your consistent posting schedule in mind

Cyber PR®

GROUP 3: CURATE CONTENT

Like: Milk, Poultry, Fish, Beans & Eggs
Servings (Recommended Frequency):
2 - 3 out of every 10 posts

Content may be King, but content curation
is Queen!

GROUP 2: SHINE A LIGHT ON OTHERS

Like: Fruits & Vegetables
Servings (Recommended Frequency):
2 - 3 out of every 10 posts

Take all of the attention off of you and
put it into others. People will
appreciate this because you are
recognizing them in front of new
potential fans and followers.

SUMMARY: Choose from Group
engaging people easily and natura

MEDIA PYRAMID

GROUP 5: SHINING A LIGHT ON YOURSELF

(AKA SELF PROMOTION)
Like: Fats, Oils & Sweets (Use Sparingly!)
Servings (Recommended Frequency):
1 out of every 10 posts

OK to do, but not too often! Don't forget about your specific calls to action or they won't be fruitful!

GROUP 4: A PICTURE SAYS 1,000 WORDS

Like: Milk, Cheese & Yogurt
Servings (Recommended Frequency):
2 out of every 10 posts

Visuals are extremely effective and mix up your strategy nicely. Take photos with your mobile, and post them directly to Facebook and Twitter.

GROUP 1: DIRECT ENGAGEMENT

Like: Bread, Cereal & Pasta
Servings (Recommended Frequency):
3 - 4 out of every 10 posts

Make sure you're in a two-way conversation with people constantly.

and mix it up. Soon you will be fully
without thinking! Just like Eating!

CHAPTER 2: *Facebook*

A. ROOM ONE IN YOUR SOCIAL MEDIA HOUSE

Fan-Tastic Facebook Facts

- More than 1 billion people worldwide are currently on Facebook.

- It's the 2nd most popular site on the Internet following Google.

- 60 percent (more than 600 million) Facebook users log in daily

- 20 minutes is the average amount of time spent per visit

- 58 percent of users are female, 42 percent male

- 140 is the average number of friends on a Personal Page

- 680 million mobile users

- 1 out of every 5 page views online

It goes without saying that you need to get your Facebook marketing strategy organized and working to your benefit.

My Cyber PR® team and I have written so many "how to" articles on Facebook and the site gets easier to use as it develops, while the articles get shorter and easier to craft. That being said, at the time of this printing in spring 2013, Facebook has changed so many times it's hard to keep up.

I'm betting Facebook will change yet again even after this book gets released, so please bear that in mind as you read this.

Facebook is still a bit like quicksand under our feet when it comes to music promotion, and you have to stay on top of the changes as they get released.

FACEBOOK QUESTION I GET ASKED EVERY SINGLE TIME I SPEAK

Musician: Do I really need to have a Facebook personal profile as well as a Facebook Fan Page?

Me: The answer is YES!

HERE'S WHY

1. You Need to Have a Personal Profile in Order to Administer Your Fan Page.

2. Personal Pages Max Out at 5,000 Friends.

This means if you friend more than 5,000 people, bands, and brands on your personal profile, you will have to unfriend people in order to add new ones, or start another personal profile (which Facebook does not consider "legal"). So, having a Fan Page is crucial, because it allows you have to have more than 5,000 friends.

3. You Can Not Track Facebook Insights (Analytics) From a Personal Profile. Knowing the effectiveness of your marketing is vital to improving your reach and your marketing. You cannot measure this from a personal profile.

4. Some Things Really Are Personal.

Facebook is now an important tool for many of our non-musical/self-promoting friends. Some people in your life may want to share with you and your family, tag photos of you in personal settings, etc. These friends may not care so much about your Fan Page updates, song giveaways and tour announcements. There is now a way to separate what is truly private more effectively than ever before (See Using Lists on Your Personal Profile).

HOW YOU ARRIVED AT THIS PROBLEM

You may have started promoting yourself on Facebook before Facebook Fan Pages were released, so your Facebook fans and your "real" friends are muddled together.

I'm not implying that your fans are not your "real" friends; I'm just saying there is probably a separation that you make, and what you share with each group may be different.

This can be problematic because now, all of the sudden, you want to add your music information on your Personal Page. While you're also cross-posting information on your Fan Page, you find yourself doubling up on your work, while possibly annoying your Aunt Matilda and your Uncle Bob.

SHOULD YOU HAVE FANS ON YOUR PERSONAL PROFILE?

I believe that having a true, intimate relationship with your fans can be a powerful way of making them your biggest advocates and cheerleaders. However, you may feel uncomfortable sharing your daughter's kindergarten photos with your fans that know you in a different context. This is a personal decision that I can't make for you. It's up to you to share what feels comfortable.

MAKE PERSONAL UPDATES *STAY* PERSONAL
Using Lists on Your Personal Profile

By using Facebook's lists, you can select exactly who will (or won't) be able to view each status update. This can be a godsend if you have been confused about what is appropriate to share versus what you consider truly private.

Create a list of your family, friends, co-workers or anyone else you want to group together. When you make a post, you can choose to have only that list of people view certain status updates.

By utillizing these lists, you will effectively make your personal profile "private" so that none of your fans (or anyone who isn't currently a "friend" of yours) will be able to view any of your status updates.

In addition, Facebook lists can be used as an effective technique for converting new fans who come across your personal profile.

Apply a list to all of your status updates except for ONE public status update, which will be a link and an announcement that all of your music related content will be available on your Fan Page (don't forget to include a link). This way any new fans that come across your Fan Page will only see one status update with directions on how to connect with you further so the muddling of friends and fans can stop now!

B. FIVE WAYS NOT TO ACHIEVE SUCCESS ON FACEBOOK

If you are anything like the majority of people, artists, authors, entrepreneurs and beyond who have built a Facebook fan page, then I'm sure you've noticed something... Facebook makes it ALMOST impossible to make any sort of real growth happen.

A recent study reported by Mashable (from Napkin Labs), showed that on average only 6% of fans engage with a brand's Facebook page:

On average, just 6% of fans engage with a brand's Facebook Page via likes, comments, polls and other means, according to a study from Napkin Labs, a Facebook app developer that works with brands and agencies. Of those fans that did, the average engagement was the equivalent of less than one like over the course of the eight weeks the study was conducted.

There are several reasons for this. Most of these, truthfully, are human error which we will discuss below. But there is no doubt that Facebook is taking strides to make it more difficult for you to achieve growth & impressions on their platform.

The problem at hand is akin to a common proverb: "Teach a man to fish and he eats for a lifetime..." However, in the case of Facebook, it's more like, once you teach the man to fish, you then put a thick layer of ice over the water, making it FAR more difficult for him to catch anything.

Let's dive into the issues at hand below.

You Don't Pay. Period.

This is the proverbial "ice over the water." No matter what you do to correct your own understanding of how Facebook works, and implement a more effective strategy, you WILL have to deal with the fact that Facebook uses an algorithm that works in the favor of advertisers. The money that advertisers spend on Facebook grants them first access through the ice to all of the fish in the sea.

A friend of mine, technologist Marcus Whitney, explained the dilemma here beautifully in a recent panel he spoke on with me for AIMP at ASCAP in Nashville (as reported by Music Row):

"Of Facebook's $1.53 billion in revenue, 95% of what they earned was in advertising and 25% of that was from mobile ads. You used to be able to reach 100% of the people that liked your page on FB, but now you can at max reach 15% of them without paying."

At the end of the day, Facebook is catering to their customers. Believe it or not, Facebook's customers are not YOU. They are the advertisers. They are the people willing to spend money to be connected with others, and this algorithm was created to ensure that this happens.

Facebook has created an option for those of us who are NOT full-time advertisers, that for better or worse, gives the opportunity to "gain access to fish in the sea" more quickly and effectively. This is the dreaded "promoted post" function that Facebook introduced recently. By paying even as little as $15, you are FAR more likely to see true engagement happen on your posts, simply because Facebook is ALLOWING this to happen (because you've paid for it!).

As ridiculous as this seems, this option does present you with a good opportunity to jumpstart the engagement of a new page by promoting select posts that nurture strong engagement with your audience.

Jon Ostrow and I tested this over the holiday season last winter with one promoted post and here were our results:

With just $15 spent, we received 46 likes, 237 comments and most importantly (for the purpose of this "algorithm" conversation), the number of people who SAW the post was 4,517… A whopping 10 TIMES the number of our average post.

But even with this great response from the one promoted post, it would have meant nothing had we not been prepared to leverage the new engagement through a strong strategy. This strategy is the piece that so many are missing. This is the human error mentioned above. Here are five things that will sabotage your success on Facebook:

1. You Don't Post Consistent, Compelling Content (CCC)

This means that your content is not only consistent in terms of the style and theme, but in terms of frequency as well. A well run Facebook fan page should have one post per day (two if you are getting great engagement) and the content should be varied enough to keep it interesting but similar enough that it helps to develop your overall brand.

2. You Don't Use Mixed Media

Facebook is not Twitter. Text isn't the answer to success on Facebook. Facebook has acknowledged the fact that people are more likely to engage with photos, videos and links than they are simple, standard text updates. Facebook gives these types of posts more weight in their algorithm.

3. You Don't Focus on Community

Facebook is a SOCIAL network. It is not a broadcast tool. If you spend your time on Facebook telling people about yourself over and over again like a broken record rather than asking, conversing and building real relationships, you'll miss out on what Facebook actually has to offer. Find ways that your fans can not only interact with you, but can interact with each other, and you'll really start to see some magic happen on your page as well.

4. You Don't RE-Engage Your Community / AKA You Only Engage ONCE

It is one thing to ask questions to your fans on Facebook, or to share compelling content that warrants comments, questions, etc. – but it is entirely different for you to RE-engage your community by responding to each comment and question. It is this re-engagement of your community that will keep them coming back, helping them to build stronger loyalty to your brand. Oh... and all of this will help you to rank higher in the algorithm.

It is a snowball effect, the better you perform, the more weight your posts will hold in FB's algorithm, and the more people will see your posts and engage with them...

5. You Don't Pay Attention to Analytics

It is shocking how many people ignore the fact that Facebook actually GIVES you detailed analytics on your fan page. They do this for a reason! (See: the snowball effect above in #4).

Facebook's Insights give you a detailed look at who your fan base is, where they live, and most importantly, what content they are most willing to engage with. Your content strategy never needs to be a static thing – it should be fluid! It should shape-shift as you find out more about who your fans are and what their needs are. Using Facebook Insights is critical to a strong Facebook fan page that holds well in Facebook's algorithm.

Of course, using Facebook Insights are only helpful if you know what the average metrics on Facebook are, so that you can compare your efforts to the standard.

First off, you have to understand the average number of fans on a Facebook page... this will help you establish a realistic goal to work for.

C. SIX SHOCKING REASONS FACEBOOK FANS LACK ENGAGEMENT

A vast majority of social media users are unaware of just how difficult growth of a Facebook fan page can actually be. This fact is not meant to scare you away from building your community on Facebook; the purpose is to shine a light on the harsh reality that is Facebook-centric community building. I sincerely hope that you use the following information for good: to set more realistic goals, put more effective strategies in place, and build stronger fan communities.

1. Average Life of a Facebook Post

One common complaint about the Internet in general by new users (or non-users) is that they don't like the idea that something published online "lives forever." Well, fret not... because this couldn't be further from the truth.

Yes, your content will technically be online, but the average lifespan of a Facebook post is just a short three hours. This means that after the average three-hour timespan, your Facebook posts will no longer show up in any of your fans' news feeds.

Although three minutes is actually a far higher number than, say, Twitter (see: 18 minutes of fame), this does mean that you MUST understand when your fans are online and most likely to engage with your posts so that each day you post in your most effective three-hour window.

2. Percentage of Total Fan Base Willing to Engage with a Brand Page

Mashable covered a recent study by Napkin Labs that exposed the shocking statistic that only 6% of a total fan base will ever actually engage with a brand page:

On average, just 6% of fans engage with a brand's Facebook Page via likes, comments, polls and other means, according to a study from Napkin Labs, a Facebook app developer that works with brands and agencies. Of those fans that did, the average engagement was the equivalent of less than one like over the course of the eight weeks the study was conducted.

While this does fuel the fire of the argument that you need more fans – A LOT more fans – in order to build any sort of community on your Facebook page, this study actually contributes to the idea of having 1,000 true fans.

The fact that 6% of a total fan base will engage with a brand page is partially because of Facebook's algorithm… Facebook's Edge Rank algorithm is a system that ranks and displays only the most relevant and important content on your news feed from your friends and pages you have liked. But the issue of your fan base lacking engagement also has a lot to do with the fact that the overwhelming majority of the average fan base is made up of Ambient or even Engaged fans, and not the kind of Super Fans needed to truly build a consistently engaged community.

3. Average Engagement Rate

As scary as the 6% stat above is, this one gets even more frightening… There have been several recent studies done on the actual average engagement rate of a page (the 'People Talking About This Page' number) and it is shown that the average engagement rate of a fan page is only 0.96% (yes, that's less than 1%).

THIS MEANS: Anything above a 1% engagement is considered strong, results-wise.

The difference between this stat and the one above (See #2) is that the number above reflects the percentage of fans who are EVER willing to engage with a page over the lifetime of the relationship. In other words, for the average fan page, 94% of your fans never have nor will they ever engage.

Meanwhile, this stat reflects the true engagement of a fan page on Facebook's rolling seven-day scale. In other words, within seven days (on average), the number of "People Talking About This Page" divided by the number of "Total Fans" will equal around 1%.

4. Posting Less Will Garner Stronger Results

After seeing these stats, the natural reaction is to want to publish content even MORE often to do everything you can to build this number higher than a measly 1%, right? Well… sorry, but that won't work either. Further studies from several sources have shown that the sweet-spot of 1-2 posts per day on Facebook fan page will garner the strongest results. Anything more than that and you will actually start to see diminishing results.

5. You Will Be Published For Being Efficient

Because consistency is key to a strong social media strategy, it is critical that you publish content every single day. No breaks.

Even though you should only post one (or possibly two) posts per day, this can get overwhelming quickly. But thankfully there are several apps, such as Hootsuite, that allow you to schedule content for Facebook ahead of time.

PHEW… Great News!

Don't get too excited just yet. Let's see what Facebook's Edge Rank algorithm has to say about this…

Unfortunately, a study by Hubspot has shown that publishing content from any 3rd party (yes, including Hootsuite) will average a whopping 67% lower engagement rate than content published directly to Facebook.

Good News: Facebook HAS introduced a way to publish content ahead of time using their own platform.

Do to so, go to your fan page, click the Status Update box, and click the little clock icon and add in the date and time you'd like to publish each post.

6. Likelihood of Posts going Viral on Facebook

We have all seen those photos, memes or videos that have gone viral in the past. And understandably so, this idea of "going viral" is why many people started using social media to promote themselves or their brand in the first place. Well, we're sorry to say that it look's like Facebook's Edge Rank algorithm has reared it's ugly head once again.

The Edge Rank algorithm is a system that ranks and displays only the most 'relevant' and 'important' content on your news feed from your friends and pages you have liked... Not that it has EVER been easy to 'go viral' online, and the fact remains that most viral videos, photos and memes do so because of chance. There IS NO science behind viral content. But with that said, Facebook doesn't make it easy for this type of viral reaction to ever happen to content published from a Fan page.

In the suite of Facebook Insights data (Facebook's native analytics tools given to all Facebook fan page admins) there is a stat called "virality" which is the percentage of fans who have shared your content on their own timelines for their own friends, family and fans to see.

A recent study from Edge Rank Checker shows that as of March 4th, 2013, the average "virality" rate of a post on Facebook fan page only 1.5%. This means that of your 100 fans, only 1.5 of them (on average) will share the content with their communities.

D. HOW TO MAKE A FRIENDS LIST

1. While looking at your timeline, you should see a left side bar with your name and profile picture on top. Under that timeline, find your "Friends" menu (If you don't see it right away, click "More").

2. After you click "Friends," you will be redirected to a page consisting of all of your friends lists. You will already have some lists based off of your friends geographic locations and other information (such as where they graduated school, employment, etc.). To create a new list of friends based off other information, click the "+ Create List" at the top of the page.

3. In the pop-up menu, simply name the list ("Super Fans," "Street Team," etc.) and type in the friends' whose names you wish to add to this list.

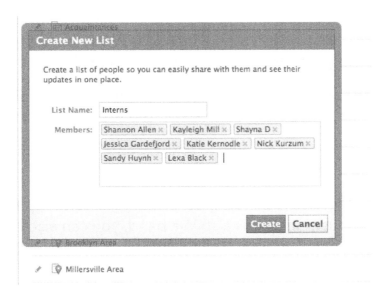

4. After the list is made, you can click on the list and see an updated News Feed of just content posted by the people within that list.

E. HOW TO CREATE A FAN PAGE

If you have been resisting this step – DO IT NOW. To be professional as an artist means having a professional Fan Page on Facebook.

STEP 1: On your home page, click Pages on the left-hand sidebar. When Pages opens, click on "Create a Page" on the top, right of the screen.

STEP 2: Click on the bottom saying "Artist, Band, or Public Figure" on the bottom, left-hand side of the screen.

STEP 3: Select "Musician/Band" (You can create as many Pages as you want. If you're a musician who is also in a band, you can also create one for yourself and one for your band.)

STEP 4: Enter your name, name your page, then select "I agree to terms and services," and click "Get Started."

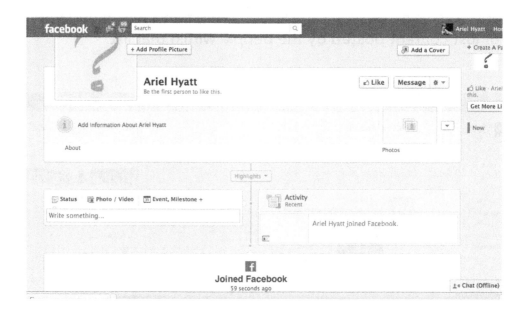

HOW TO LOCATE YOUR PAGE

This seems like a piece of information that would be fairly obvious, but it's not! It is often difficult to locate Fan Pages the first time around.

1. Click the drop-down arrow on the upper right hand side of the screen by "Home"

2. There, you should see all of the pages you manage.

3. Visit the desired page.

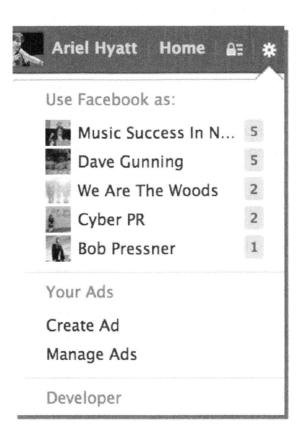

QUICKSTART GUIDE TO GET YOUR FAN PAGE SET UP CORRECTLY

1. Cover Photo – The most noticeable change on Facebook Fan Pages is the giant cover photo that artists can now implement. This was a cool feature for personal profiles and allows users to show off their creativity (or that amazing photo you took of the sunset on vacation), but it is a really powerful branding tool for artists. Uploading an eye-catching photo will help draw fans into your page and solidify your image. Branding has always been a little tricky on Facebook Fan Pages as you had to use certain apps to effectively do this, but this left the Wall essentially "unbranded." Cover photos solve this issue and bring a whole new life to the "Wall."

2. Pinning – Facebook now allows you to "pin" certain posts to the top of your Timeline. I'm particularly fond of this feature because it allows artists to keep promotional posts at the top of their page instead of endlessly posting the same promotion over and over again. Instead of continuing to post updates about an upcoming show, bands can focus on providing more interesting and engageable content to pull fans toward their page. Keeping the show's promotion pinned to the top of the page ensures all visitors will see that post and will be reminded of the show. It's a beautiful thing.

3. Highlight – You can "highlight" certain posts to make them stretch across the entire width of the Timeline. As fans scroll through your Timeline, these highlighted posts will jump out and will be sure to catch attention. Highlighting videos is a great way to get more fans to watch them, even as they fall down on the Timeline. This feature also helps draw attention to significant events that have happened throughout the band's history.

4. Milestones – The whole point of Timeline is to allow users to scroll through someone's Facebook history. This is a very powerful tool for artists. Coldplay has documented the band's entire history on their Timeline. Going so far as to show a picture of the band's first rehearsal, first show, first EP, first NYC show, etc. I'm not a huge Coldplay fan (If you are, I hope you'll still keep reading!), and even I found this very interesting. Imagine how much actual Coldplay fans love this! For new, up-and-coming bands, this is a great opportunity to let fans grow with you and celebrate all your accomplishments as they happen.

5. Unique Fan Experience – Facebook has ensured that each fan's experience on an artist's Timeline will be unique. What does this mean? It means that when I visit Coldplay's Timeline, I see what my friends are saying about Coldplay, whether or not they actually posted on Coldplay's Timeline. For example, Cyber PR® team member, Jon Ostrow, posted about Coldplay back in August, and because Jon and I are friends and interact frequently, his post shows up high on Coldplay's Timeline for me. This feature will intensify the sense of community your fans experience on your Fan Page.

6. Messages – One of the most exciting features of Timeline is messaging. This has long been a desire for Fan Page admins, and Facebook has found a way to deliver without allowing Fan Pages to spam their fans. Fan Pages can now receive messages from personal profiles and then respond to them. This allows a whole new level of interaction with your fans. The only limitation is Fan Pages can't initiate the direct message process, they can only receive messages.

7. Admin Panel – It's not all about the fan's experience; Facebook has made it easier for admins with the newest version of its "admin" panel. In the admin panel, you can easily see new notifications, new likes and a basic insight graph. The "Build Audience" tab makes it easy for admins to grow the number of likes. You can use the age-old "Invite Friends" technique (obviously not a new feature, but now easier to find). And now you can also send out invites from your email contacts. This is a great feature that can be extremely helpful for artists with a large email list and for new artists who have a large personal email list.

8. Landing Page – This isn't really a feature, instead it's more of an omission. Facebook has, unfortunately, taken away the ability to assign different landing pages on Timeline. But, there is a way to work around this. The various artist pages have unique URLs. You can now give fans this URL and send them directly to where you keep your music and email sign up form. While this isn't as good as a default landing page, the added benefits of Timeline and the new layouts of most of the artist pages more than make up for this (in my humble opinion).

Since the initial launch of Timeline for Fan Pages, brands have seen a significant increase in engagement (as much as 46 percent). This stat is huge and it's vital for artists to take advantage of this increased engagement while it lasts. However, the new Timeline won't do the work for you - you have to get in there and make it happen.

It's now more important than ever that artists push out quality and engaging content. Know what you want your "brand image" to be, and post content accordingly.

F. HOW TO INCLUDE CONTENT IN STATUS UPDATES

Post - The following box appears on your "Wall." There are three icons in this box which will allow you to post different content with your fans.

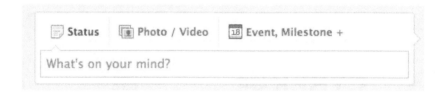

Let's go over each of the buttons from left to right:

Status - After clicking "status," a box will appear where you can place your text and then the "Post" button must be clicked in order to display this information to all your fans (everyone who "Likes" your Page).

Photo/Video - Posting photos and videos helps musicians connect with fans on an entirely different level. Once you've clicked the "Photo/Video" tab, two items will appear: "Upload Photo/Video" and "Create Photo Album."

Event/Milestone - This is another unique feature that Facebook now offers on Fan Pages. "Event/Milestone" allows you to do several things. "Event" allows you to create events in which you can invite as many guests as you please. "Milestone" allows you to create a previous event that has made a great impact; you name the event, state the location, when it happened, and tell the story. And "Question" allows you to ask your fans about a specific question or create a poll (with up to three options) for your fans to take. This is a powerful tool that helps you engage more with your fans.

HOW TO MAKE YOUR FACEBOOK TIMELINE POP!

There is a fabulous feature that will help you highlight the things that happen throughout your life and career that you can post onto your Facebook Fan Page.

This is a phenomenal tool for going back in time and recording important things in the history of your personal life, your band life, or anything else you might like to have highlighted.

For artists that have histories with other bands, this is doubly amazing because you can go back and create milestones for practically anything, and really build your story.

HERE ARE A FEW THINGS YOU CAN ADD

- Past tour dates
- Past album release dates (with album cover image)
- Past press placements & radio ad dates
- The day you saw an amazing concert that inspired you
- The day you were signed to a label
- The day you were dropped from a label
- The day you got your publishing deal
- The day you recorded your first song
- The day you entered the studio
- The day you had your first vocal lesson

FACEBOOK IS ALWAYS CHANGING
But the Basic Rules of Creating Consistent, Compelling Content Won't

You have already learned how to mix content and how often you should post. Please refer back to the Social Media Food Pyramid for step-by-step instructions on that in chapter one.

Here are eight more ideas for you:

1. Like Other People's Stuff

But don't stop there! Leave real comments that are thoughtful and note-worthy.

2. Ask Questions

Ask easy questions that people can weigh in on like, "What's your favorite music to clean your house to?" or, "What's the most annoying jingle of all time?" or, "What's your favorite movie for crying?" etc. People can easily answer things that they have emotional connections to. This is a smart way to get fans involved.

3. Wish People a Happy Birthday (This is from your personal profile, but it's a considerate way to appreciate people, especially fans.)

TIP: Create a great Happy Birthday video of you/your band singing and post that on every single person's Timeline who has a birthday.

4. Photo Themes

How about a church of the week, plate of French fries of the week or a thing that makes you LOL each week? Having a theme that people can recognize and comment on can be a way to have people expect great content from you.

5. Photo Contests

Don't just stop at posting and sharing photos. Why not hold a contest of favorite photos from your hometown, or of your pet, or of your favorite food, etc. We love a service called One Kontest, and for a fee, they can help you run a fantastic photo contest with your fans.

6. Video Curation

Pick something that goes with your aesthetics – or a great video from the '70s , '80s or '90s, commercials from your childhood, moments in sports history you remember – anything that is meaningful to you may be meaningful to your fans as well.

7. Spotify Playlists

Create playlists everyone can contribute to and share them on your Fan Page. Songs about tennis, songs about broken hearts or songs to play while driving with the top down – there are a million themes.

8. This Day In History

Are you into art or theatre or great rock and roll history? Post photos and videos!

SEVEN STEPS TO CREATE AN EVENT ON YOUR FAN PAGE

STEP 1: Log in to Facebook

STEP 2: Go to your Fan Page and click "Event, Milestone +"
(it's at the top of your timeline)

STEP 3: Next, click "Event"

STEP 4: Enter all the appropriate information in the "Event" box and click "create"

STEP 5: Select your guests once the event has been created under "Who's invited?"

STEP 6: Select an eye-catching event photo by clicking "add event photo"

STEP 7: Once you have chosen an event photo, click "create."

Now that your event has the information, photo, and guests, you may now "share" it with friends. This event will now display on your page and allow you to post comments about it.

FIVE STEPS TO CREATE A MILESTONE ON YOUR TIMELINE

Anything that was important in the history of your band, your life and your music can be added as a milestone.

STEP 1: Login to Facebook, go to the Status/Post Bar and click milestone

STEP 2: A box will appear. Input all the information – Fill out the event name/location and date

STEP 3: Tell a story about the milestone/Why was it significant?

STEP 4: Add any photos that relate to the milestone

STEP 5: Click save and your milestone will be published on your timeline

TIP #1: Make sure when you create a milestone to add a photo, a little story or blurb, or a link to another site that helps to tell the story of that particular milestone. Now your entire Timeline will be robust and look amazing!

TIP #2: If you are going to be adding multiple milestones at once, I suggest that you check the box that says "hide from your newsfeed" so that your fans do not receive a whole bunch of notifications at once.

G. HOW TO GET LIKES ON YOUR PAGE

In order to increase the "Likes" on your Fan Page, you must invite more people to "like" your page. This is a very simple process!

First, click the tab "Build Audience" in the top right. Once you've clicked that, "Invite Friends..." will appear right below it.

After you've clicked that tab, a box labeled "Suggest <NAME OF YOUR PAGE> to friends" with all of your friends from your personal profile will appear.

Click on each friend individually and then click "submit". This will send an individual invitation to each person to become a fan of your Page.

That's it!

H. FACEBOOK APPS

WHAT ARE APPS?

Apps (short for applications) are tools created by outside developers that intergrate into Facebook. You can add apps to your Fan Page so you can display features such as music, photos, tour dates, links to other social media sites and videos for a fully customized experience. Apps are also developed for smartphones and tablets (such as iPads), and are the main reasons they have both become wildly popular.

Thousands of developers create apps for countless uses. There are so many, your head may spin. For example, My Band is an app developed by ReverbNation that allows you to put a skinnable tab and page displaying music videos and more on your Facebook Fan Page.

Facebook has a great page that explains how to help you with apps. FAQ's are here: http://bit.ly/facebook-apps-faq

THE THREE TOP FACEBOOK APPS FOR MUSICIANS

Here are my top Facebook apps for musicians along with links to where you can download them. These are all effective and all quite similar, so just choose one so you do not confuse your fans with multiple music pages. Search in the App store to find all of these on Facebook.

1. Music By ReverbNation

Musicians, artists, and bands can post unlimited songs for streaming or download, add bios and band photos, sell music and have friends add music to share with their friends. This app also includes links to your home page and you can add up to 30 of your songs (full-length) to your Facebook Fan Page.

2. BandPage

Bandpage used to be called RootMusic. They have two versions: a free and a paid option ($1.99 /mo or $19.99/yr). You don't have to know any code or HTML to put together a branded, professional looking page. They have integrated their BandPage technology with many of the functions built into Facebook, making it a great option for pimping out your Facebook Page. You can also add widgets to give away tracks in exchange for email addresses (they call it "gating"). You can also add SoundCloud and Twitter straight onto your page.

BandPage has recently launched an incredible new part of their service called BandPage Experiences. These are micro funding opportunities that you can add on, such as coming to a VIP event before or after the show, setting up a Skype with your fans, or selling a fun merchant item. This is an amazing way to put money in your pocket without launching a full on crowdfunding campaign. BandPage has listed multiple fabulous opportunities that artists are showcasing here: http://www.bandpage.com/fans. Visit the page, have a peek around, and get inspired!

3. Fanbridge

Fanbridge helps you engage, reward, and grow your fans. It gives your fans the tools and incentives to convert their friends to fans. Identify and reward your top influencers. You can find Fanbridge in the App store on Facebook or here: http://www.fanbridge.com/

FIVE MORE USEFUL APPS TO TRY

To locate the following four apps to install on your page, search for them in the app store: http://bit.ly/FaceBookAppStore

1. BandsinTown

Bandsintown lets your fans know when and where you are playing. Bandsintown has the ability to find the shows your band has booked and create events for those shows for you.

Once the events are created, you can promote each show through Facebook (and whatever social network you have Facebook connected to).

These posts are built with tags geared towards touring artists, so you can stipulate whether each show is pre-sale, on sale, sold out, etc. It also gives you the embed code so you can post your tour dates on your website or blog. It also syncs with Twitter, and WordPress (via a WordPress plugin).

On top of all this syncing brilliance, for an extra fee, Bandsintown has a deal with MobBase to help you get your own iPhone/Android app preconfigured with your tour dates, tickets, and events from Bandsintown.

2. YouTube

Everyone loves videos, and YouTube is the universally recognized icon for videos. All three music pages have video plug ins, so a YouTube button can be a great way to showcase videos

3. Poll Daddy

Poll Daddy features both private polls that only your friends can see, and public ones that you can share with all of your fans. This is a great way to poll your fan base and see what they really want!

4. Ustream.TV

Ustream is the leading live, interactive broadcast platform that enables anyone with Internet connection and a camera to engage their audience in a meaningful, immediate way. You can broadcast your performances from your shows, or even from your living room in real time. If you are looking to get involved with this forward thinking technology, don't forget to make your actions available to your social networks. Check out this app to embed your Ustream activity right onto your Facebook Fan Page! http://tinyurl.com/FBUstream

5. Woobox

Woobox has great Pinterest, Youtube and Instagram apps that allow you to show your boards, photos and videos on your Facebook page by adding them as an app box (the boxes that appear under your timeline image). The extra benefit here is you keep fans on your Facebook Fan Page instead of taking them to another social site.

1. Go to http://woobox.com

2. Scroll all the way to the bottom and click the type of app you want (they also have paid apps to try for coupons and contests)

3. This will take you to your Facebook page, with a popup. Click "Go to App."

I. FACEBOOK ADVERTISING

By now you have suggested your Fan Page to all of your friends and you still don't see the lift in numbers you want. It might be time to take out a Facebook ad. They have been around for years now and are constantly growing in popularity – because they work to drive new fans to like your Page. The following are two ad options for Facebook we recommend.

ReverbNation's Promote It

ReverbNation has an affordable, artist-friendly Facebook ad-buying program called Promote It, which is enticing due to its targeted research surrounding your ad and how quick it is to actually set up.

The Promote It tool utilizes a framework built off thousands of beta tests by 10,000 artists and 18,000 campaigns, so it's road-tested. This tool is set up to create an effective ad for you by asking your comparisons, targeting demographics and more, with little effort. This allows ReverbNation to create a stellar campaign for you. Check out this short video that dives deeper into the effectiveness and quickness of using ReverbNation's Promote It: http://bit.ly/ReverbPromoteIt

Go DIY Directly with Facebook

For a nominal fee, you can purchase an ad that is extremely niche-targeted so only users within the demographics you determine can view the ad. By advertising a page within Facebook, your ad will include a "Like" button so that users can "like" your page without having to click through the ad. Having fewer steps to get users to become fans can make your ad campaign far more effective.

Facebook also allows you to monitor your ad so you can see how it is performing and make adjustments as necessary. In the ad manager area, you can download advertising performance state, responder demographics, and responder profiles anytime so you can correct and continue as you hone your ad campaign.

HOW TO CREATE AN EFFECTIVE FACEBOOK AD

STEP 1: Design Your Ad

1. Scroll to the bottom of any page on Facebook and click the link that says "Advertising" and click on the green box that says "Create An Ad". This begins your creation of the ad by directing you to the "Design" area.

2. Next, select your Fan Page under the "Destination" dropbox menu. For the type, choose "Facebook Ads", and for the "Destination Tab" determine which landing page on your Fan Page you want users to be directed to once they click your ad.

3. You cannot change the title of your ad and it automatically becomes the name of your Facebook Fan Page you are advertising. For the body of your ad, you are limited to 135 characters so you must create an effective message that will drive users to your page.

TIP: Make sure the content of your ad is interesting and compelling so the user wants to "like" your page!

This should include a call to action (CTA), whether it's an invitation to your next show, or the opportunity to listen to captivating blues music.

Get creative! *(Please note: you cannot advertise a contest unless Facebook gives you permission to do so.)*

For a full list of guidelines go here: http://bit.ly/fb-guidelines1

4. The last design section asks you to upload an image. Upload the desired image of your band that is clear and represents your music and

message in the most effective manner. Remember: A picture is worth 1,000 words, or perhaps 1,000 fans!

STEP 2: Target Your Ad

Facebook allows numerous options to target your ad to your desired potential fan base. In this section, you can choose the cities and countries you desire the ad to be accessible to, and also further disseminate by country and city. Select the age range and sex of your target demographic. The next section asks you to target the interest of your potential fans. It is extremely important to make sure you include music and your genre so your ad appears to users with similar musical interests.

STEP 3: Campaigns, Pricing, and Scheduling

This is where you set the amount you want to pay for the ad. First, choose the appropriate currency and time zone from the drop down menu. You then set your budget by either "Day" or by "Lifetime Budget". If you select "Day", you enter the maximum amount you want to spend for that day, and if you choose "Lifetime Budget" you type in what you want to spend for the entire campaign. You are also given the option to pay by impressions under the Pricing area (this would be how many people view your ad and is not measured by clicks). The default is to pay per click (this means you are charged each time a user clicks on your ad). Then select the Scheduled Dates of how long you want to run your ad. To accurately measure how your fan base increases, set it for at least a month.

STEP 4: Review Your Ad

The last section is where you review your Facebook Ad and approve it – once approved by you, and then Facebook, your ad launches and you are well on your way to building your fan base!

Using either method will help to increase your Facebook fan base, but make sure you are doing your part by posting REGULARLY and ENGAGING your current fans and potential fans to make sure they stay interested and connected with you. If someone clicks on a Facebook ad, goes to your Fan Page and notices you are not active, I would not blame them for not becoming your fan. By using a Facebook ad in conjunction with your awesome and active Fan Page, you will definitely see an increase in your fan base.

J. USING SOCIAL MEDIA TO DRIVE RESULTS: RDIO & SPOTIFY

The old way dictates that bands and musicians need to get radio airplay. The formula was simple. Get as much radio airplay as you humanly could, saturate the market, drive people to stores to purchase the CD, go on tour, sell the tickets, and win big.

For any of you who have spent money on radio campaigns, as independent artists, without extremely deep pockets and major label support, you probably ended up losing a fortune. And aside from a few radio chart reports, you probably had very little to show for your expensive radio campaign.

The new music business says it's all about social media and making as many friends as you can across prevalent social media platforms. You do this by driving those friends to your mailing list; creating a mailing list that goes out regularly with consistent calls to action so you can track your effectiveness.

As you can see, these two models are quite disparate - but each can work in different ways.

HOW TO CONNECT TERRESTRIAL RADIO & SOCIAL MEDIA

Here is how you turn terrestrial radio plays into social media effectiveness. Note: you will see that radio is slow to adapt to social media and a good amount of radio stations and specialty shows will be difficult to find on social media. This is the most frustrating scenario. However, with some perseverance, you should be able to garner results using this system.

Step 1: Look at the radio report under the most recent date to see what stations have started playing your single (also known as "adding" the single). If a station has added a song, there will be a number in the space corresponding to the station letters and the date.

Step 2: Copy and paste the station's call letters (like WSLC) into the Facebook search box and hit "Search."

Step 3: Repeat on Twitter, making sure that you are searching people and not tweets. Initially it will show you tweets, but it shows people results on the right side of the page. Hit "view all" in the people results.

Step 4: If you get no hits, include the town name in the search and try again.

Step 5: If no hits, you can also use the station name (like "The Mix"). The report gives the station name sometimes, but you'll most likely have to Google the call letters and frequency (i.e. WSLC 104.7) to find the name. See if you can find links to any social media on the station's page. Otherwise, search the name and frequency within Facebook and Twitter.

Step 6: If no hits, the station probably does not have any social media. Don't worry, several tiny stations don't.

Step 7: Of course, if you do find the station and the locations match, go ahead and follow them and like their pages.

Step 8: On Twitter, send an @ message thanking the station for playing your song. On Facebook, leave a comment on their page or wall.

RDIO & SPOTIFY: THE ALTERNATIVE TO TRADITIONAL RADIO

Rdio and Spotify are on-demand subscription streaming music services. For those of you familiar with Pandora, they are not the same as that service.

Pandora, like radio, enables you to passively listen to streaming music, without choosing which specific songs you want to hear. Rdio, alternatively, is an on-demand service, which means you can pick what song or album you want to listen to, and listen to it at that exact moment on your computer, mobile device or even in your car (among many other devices).

What makes Rdio and Spotify special is that they are also large social networks built solely upon music, and what people are listening to. This is where you will find people who love music. It's the only reason they use the service: to listen to music and socialize around it!

HOW TO GET YOUR MUSIC ON RDIO AND SPOTIFY

Rdio and Spotify do not do direct deals with artists at this time, so you will need to make sure your distributor has enrolled you in distribution to Rdio and Spotify. All important indie distributors can distribute your music to both platforms, including CD Baby and Tunecore.

You may also notice that in using other social applications (such as Facebook, Twitter, Soundtracking, Turntable and others) that Rdio and Twitter are integrated. In other words, when you tweet a song from Rdio, anyone can click your tweet and they will see the Rdio player. Anyone can click on that player, but only subscribers and anyone using Rdio's initial free version can hear the full song.

K. FACEBOOK & SPOTIFY

By driving social distribution and engagement among fans, Spotify can help albums reach their potential audiences more rapidly and meaningfully than ever before. The reason Spotify has grown like wildfire is because it's so easy to seamlessly share Spotify music with Facebook friends, and view their published playlists. With "Play" buttons throughout the site, it's easy to get fans to listen and interact. Spotify allows fans to listen to music straight from their Facebook personal pages without having to go to any other site (if you share a track on your Fan Page it will pop Spotify open and fans can listen to it on the Spotify platform).

Spotify currently has over 24 million active users. Your friends and fans will easily be able to see your music in their Facebook Timelines and share collaborative playlists with you, adding a level of engagement, using the most powerful glue that holds us all together—music.

SPOTIFY PLAYLISTS

A Spotify playlist is a collection of tracks grouped together and saved for easy access by you and your followers. Think of it as a modern-day mix tape where you can create a playlist for anywhere and anytime. A single playlist can store up to 10,000 tracks, and they are sharable on Facebook.

Spotify believes that sharing is a fundamental aspect of enjoying and discovering music. With this in mind, they have developed collaborative playlists to help you spread the love. This means that not only are you able to share playlists with others, you can let them edit the shared playlists as well.

L. ANALYTICS FOR FACEBOOK

SOME CAUTIONARY WORDS ABOUT ANALYTICS

You may hear that a marketing campaign is only as good as your ability to measure it.

I do agree with this on some level. It is important to measure. However, I have been to many industry panel discussions about analytics and I have studied a lot of platforms that track and measure them.

A word of caution: Just because we now have access to the data whenever anyone mentions us, visits our sites, comments, or "likes" something, does not mean you have to take action on every incident.

In fact, many pieces of your analytics will be un-actionable. That's okay. Your job, and goal around analytics, is to just observe them, respond and jump into the conversation if, and when, you can but:

Don't - worry about thanking someone every time they give you a "like" on Facebook.

Do - engage in two-way conversations with people and contribute when you can. This is not only polite, but it's also a great social media strategy!

The big picture is this: Long-term analysis of your analytics means you can begin to spot trends. You will see what is effective for you (what gets reactions) versus what is not (gets little to no reaction), and this may be a lot of things...

I suggest when you look at your analytics overtime to create a spreadsheet of the spikes you receive and write down what happened that caused them. After some time, you will begin to see patterns that can help you create more spikes and therefore better engagement.

The Takeaway: Know what your audience focuses on and how they respond to your posts.

FACEBOOK INSIGHTS

Facebook Insight is the analytics tool built into the back-end of Facebook. It's free and easy to use. It won't track Personal Pages, only Fan Pages (yet another reason to have a Fan Page). If you are the admin to your Fan Page - which you should be - you can gain access to Insight.

HOW TO ACCESS FACEBOOK INSIGHTS

STEP 1: Log in to Facebook

STEP 2: Go here: http://www.facebook.com/insights

You will now see that Insight highlights three areas: 1. your fans, 2. your interactions, and 3. your post quality.

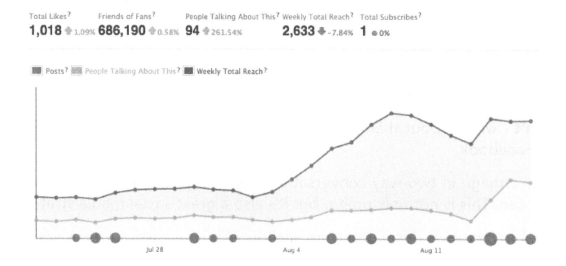

Facebook Insights dive in pretty deep and measure your comments, wall posts, and likes.

Plus, it gives you demographics on the gender and ages of your fans, and tells you how engaging your content is to your fans overall.

The Media Consumption graphs on Facebook show you how many photos have been viewed and how many streamed videos have been watched.

GOOGLE ANALYTICS FOR FACEBOOK

Many people don't know that you can install Google Analytics onto Facebook. In order to connect the two, you need to use WebDigi's Google Analytics Link Generator for Facebook to make it work.

Their secret is your designer must include Google Analytics as an image instead of a piece of Javascript. Create an image for each page you want to track in Facebook and you can use Google Analytics for tracking the same way you track pages on your own sites.

M. ARIEL'S SOUND TAKEAWAYS

- Yes, you need to have a fan page!

- Remember that good, solid engagement on a fan page is 1% (this is why having a fully integrated social media house plan is crucial)

- Photos are the most shared item on Facebook, so share lots of them

- Take the time to pimp out your page properly; branding is everything

- Lists are fantastic when you are grouping people, and they will help you tremendously with targeting on Facebook

- Supplement your page with acts that show your other favorite social media streams and activities

- Analytics are your friend; understand how to use Facebook insights

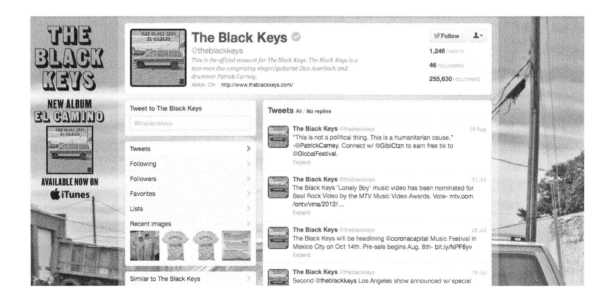

CHAPTER 3: *Twitter*

A. ROOM TWO IN YOUR SOCIAL MEDIA HOUSE

How can Twitter help musicians?

All well-known and independent musicians today have one thing in common: They use Twitter regularly, consistently, and they use it well. Here are three artists you should watch:

Amanda Palmer (@amandapalmer)

Amanda Palmer, as mentioned before, is known for her social media presence. In 2011, she managed to raise $11,000 by tweeting that she was alone on a Friday night. When she created a $25 t-shirt saying #TLOFNTC (The Losers of Friday Night on Their Computers), she raised $11,000 in two hours!

Jordan Benker (@jordanbenker)

This Berklee College of Music alum trended worldwide after promising fans he would give them a free download if they tweeted "JBenk" a million times. His fans immediately started writing tweets including "JBenk," and he got enough of them to trend worldwide.

Portugal The Man (@portugaltheman)

Portugal The Man (the band), had their equipment stolen at the 2011 Lollapalooza festival. They were able to recover the equipment after tweeting and posting on Facebook about their missing gear.

B. TWITTER IS ...

Twitter is a social site that allows you to share updates of 140 characters each. This social platform has over 280 million active users. All well-known and independent musicians today have one thing in common: They use Twitter regularly, consistently, and they use it well. And you can too.

Many people resist Twitter because they don't understand the ins and outs of it, but I promise once you master it, you will come to realize it is a fabulous way to connect with new people and potential fans. All the while, you can give your current fans even more if you take at least five minutes a day to effectively use Twitter with either your mobile or computer once you get in the groove.

Twitter is a great tool to share thoughts, ideas, tips, and advice. Even better, Twitter is great for generating awareness for a band, song, podcast, article, press release, review, and so on.

Over time, Twitter users will strengthen your bonds with fans and potential customers. If fans are interested in what you have to offer, they will react and interact. This is when Twitter becomes fun!

FIVE REASONS YOU SHOULD CARE ABOUT TWITTER

1. It's free, easy to join, and so easy to use. All you do is write small texts ("tweets") of 140 characters or less from your phone or your computer.

2. It is one of the top three social media sites (Facebook and YouTube are #1 and #2)

3. Your fan base will feel more connected to you, and they can interact directly with you via tweets, replies, and direct messages. But you don't have to follow or interact with everyone who follows you!

4. Twitter will help you build your brand. It's an amazing way to quickly connect with lots of people you'd never otherwise meet.

5. Twitter feed widgets are easy to install and you can drop them onto your own website, your Facebook Fan Page, or your blog, so your content will stay updated across all platforms.

THINGS THAT HAVE CHANGED IN MY LIFE AS A RESULT OF TWITTER

1. I Keep Up With Old Friends Consistently

Now I keep up with distant friends and feel engaged in their lives, even though we don't speak on a regular basis. I can even stay up-to-date with my best friend in Antwerp because international tweets don't get charged on my mobile phone.

2. I Save Precious Time

Because all my tweets automatically become my Facebook status updates, I don't have to constantly update two sites. Just one!

3. I Make Money!

Wendy and Lisa (of Prince/Lost Fame) became Cyber PR® clients because a friend of mine tweeted that he was meeting me in Los Angeles for coffee. Wendy and Lisa's manager read his tweet, checked out my company and called my office within hours. How cool is that?

TWITTER IN SEVEN EASY STEPS

Before you dive in, you may want to watch a great video by Common Craft that gives an easy-to-understand overview of Twitter (http://commoncraft.com/Twitter). It takes less than four minutes to watch, and sets the stage perfectly for understanding Twitter in context.

STEP 1: Think About Your Handle (User Name) First

When you go to set up an account, don't just pick a name you like. Use the name that matches your website, your Facebook profile and your other social media sites for consistency. And remember: Whatever name you choose on Twitter becomes Google-icious too.

STEP 2: Sign Up

- Go to: http://www.twitter.com

- Twitter will take you through a few sign-up steps where you'll enter your username, password, and email.

- Twitter helps you search your email address book to see if anyone you know is already using Twitter. You'll also have the option of sending email invites to your friends.

- Take some time and set up your profile properly. Put up a good profile picture because it will show up on all your tweets. Add your pitch (a few lines about you) and a link to your website. Your Twitter profile is kind of like a mini website, so take care in setting it up, just as if it were your main website.

STEP 3: Link Your Mobile Phone

Enter your cell phone number if you want to accept tweets via text message. Do this only if you have a good text messaging plan and a high tolerance for receiving large numbers of text messages on your mobile phone. You'll have the option of receiving tweets to your phone from only a few select people, so don't worry about your phone blowing up if you follow lots of people from your account. You can also edit this list down.

There are great apps you can easily install, made for any mobile device.

STEP 4: Follow Lots of People

Twitter does not work in a vacuum, so the key is to follow at least 100 people! Start by following me @CyberPR (http://twitter.com/cyberpr).

TIP: In order to find people, search for them by keyword. To do this, you will go to the grey box on the top right of the page, type topics you are interested in, words about the music you play, and so on. When you find interesting tweets in those searches, follow the people who created those tweets. This will give you a great jumping off point and an easy way to find new people to add to your followers.

STEP 5: Tweet Three Times a Day

Use the Social Media Pyramid to mix up your content and share links that your community may like.

TIP: Don't Over-Hype Yourself. If all your tweets say things like, "Buy my album! Come to my show!," you're not going to build an audience who trusts you... or wants to hear from you!

Step 6: @ People You Like! and RT

To comment on tweets you like or have a reaction to, or to connect directly with someone, just tweet @ and then their username. So if you want to say something directly to Derek Sivers, type @Sivers and then your message. This will turn up in the "Replies" section of Derek's Twitter dashboard, and he will see your comment. But so will everyone else!

This is a public message that everyone on Twitter will see.

STEP 7: Connect Directly

To send someone a direct, private message, go to the icon on the top right of your Twitter home page and in the drop down menu choose "Direct Messages." Then choose the person whom you want to send a message from the pull-down menu at the top of the page.

Direct messages are private messages. Only the user you choose can see these messages.

TIP: To send a DM, the person must be following you. If you want someone to follow you, simply @ them and ask them (9 times out of 10, they will follow you if you request)!

TWITTER BASICS: THE "HANDLE"

We are going to use my @cyberpr account as an example.

NOTE: When you follow me, you will see that Twitter will suggest other people "similar to Cyber PR." This can lead you to some more interesting people to follow.

Web Address – http://twitter.com/cyberpr

Handle – @cyberpr

Pronunciation of Handle – Say, "AT Cyber PR" (just like you say "at" when telling someone your email address.)

Reference to Handle – Say, "@CyberPR" is her "Twitter Handle."

TIP: Not everyone is going to follow you back, but a percentage will. At that point, it is your job to tweet often and frequently interact on your profile to keep your followers interested and engaged.

TWITTER DEFINITIONS

Even if you think of yourself as an intermediate or advanced Twitter user, take a quick peek at these foundational definitions.

Twitter Address - This refers to the URL where your Twitter home page is. Ex: http://twitter.com/cyberpr

Twitstream / Tweetstream / Twitter Stream – The collective stream of Twitter messages (tweets) sent by you and the people that you're following. No two people's streams are exactly alike.

Twitter Handle – This refers to your Twitter username and begins with an "@" symbol. My handle is @CyberPR.

Tweet – An individual Twitter message that is 140 characters or less. A tweet can:

> 1. Answer, "What's happening?" or just post an update
> 2. Allow you to share links to content (music, photos, blog posts, articles, or videos).
> 3. Help you engage with others by using @'s, #'s and RT's

Following – The people whose Twitter messages you follow.

Followers – The people who are following your Twitter messages.

RT (ReTweet) – Quoting or repeating someone else's tweet (Twitter message) in your tweet. This is also a significant measure of the value of a tweet; if something has been retweeted many times, it is ranked higher in the system.

@Reply – Also called "at reply," this is a tweet where your Twitter name is mentioned. This will create a public conversation between you and the other user.

DM (Direct Message) – Private tweet between you and another person. You can only send DMs to people who are following you. This is a private conversation, much like email.

Twitter Spam – Twitter messages with little or no conversational value.

Favorite – Tweet marked by you or others as favorite, as indicated by a little gold star. When you favorite something, you are adding it the list of Favorites that can be seen publicly on your profile. You are also giving feedback to the other user that their post (that you have favorited) is valuable to you in some way.

Trend – The most tweeted about words or phrases at the present time. This list is on Twitter's home page on the left. Trending topics often correspond with current events.

List – A group of users that any Twitter user can create, and then curate by trend, location, theme, and so on.

Who To Follow - Twitter will analyze the list of people that you are already following and will constantly make recommendations of other people to follow. You will find this on the left-hand side of your Twitter home page.

Listed – This section displays the lists within which you have been included by other Twitter users. You can follow entire lists here, or choose individuals to follow within these lists.

Hash Tag (#) – A hash tag is used on Twitter when people want to highlight a particular phrase, usually in reference to a topic or event. For example: #WorldCup, #MadMen, #SXSW. Common hash tag phrases that you will see on a regular basis are:

> **#FollowFriday** or **#FF** – Every Friday people send out their recommendations on who they think you should follow. Its like a public shout-out.

> **#MusicMonday** or **#MM** – Every Monday, people tweet their music recommendations.

C. HOW TO COMMUNICATE ON TWITTER

Twitter should not be used just for "status updates," (this will quickly bore your potential fans). Instead, think of Twitter as a way to communicate with others. Here are some tips for how to most effectively use Twitter to communicate with fans and friends.

TWEET SPECIFICS

At the bottom of every tweet in your Twitter stream (if you roll over it with your mouse) you will see: Expand, Reply, Retweet, Favorite. Here is what each of those directives means:

Expand

If this tweet is part of a conversation or has links or photos associated with it, pressing this will show you the entire conversation and/or links.

Reply

When you "reply" to someone, on Twitter you are, in essence, "responding" to them. Pressing the "Reply" button will make your tweet begin with "@" and the person's name (example: @CyberPr). You can mention or reply to anyone at anytime, even if you are not following him or her, or vice versa. This is a terrific way to personally communicate with fans.

ReTweet (RT)

A retweet is an action you can take that copies and pastes other people's tweets into your own Twitter timeline, but will give the original Twitter users credit where credit is due. You can RT anything: an inspirational tweet, a great link to a song, a simple thought you liked, etc.

Favorite

If you see a tweet you like (a great link, something useful, or something that makes you LOL), you can "favorite" it. Twitter will create a list of your favorite tweets that everyone will be able to see on your profile. You are essentially bookmarking tweets that you like.

HOW TO RESPOND TO SEVERAL PEOPLE AT ONCE

All you have to do is put several people's handles (usernames) at the beginning or throughout the tweet with the "@" before each of their names.

TIP: After you find potential fans on Twitter, DO NOT jump directly into self-promotion mode. Connect with them on shared interests, and learn about them. After you make a genuine connection, you will have plenty of time to plug your music! Refer to the Social Media Pyramid for an easy strategy to mix up your tweets.

D. PROACTIVELY STARTING CONVERSATIONS

There is a "Timeline" on Twitter that displays the tweets for everyone that you are following at the same time:

Many musicians sit back and wait for different @ mentions to pop up on their account. It's up to you to proactively start some "@reply" conversations.

A mundane or silly conversation can easily be started on Twitter. Last summer, I was loading the dishwasher and tweeted: When you're loading the dishwasher: Tines up or tines down?

All of a sudden, over a dozen people jumped in and told me how they loaded their dishwashers. My followers who commented back actually ended up having a lot in common with me. I ran into a few people from that tweet stream at a conference, and we joked about the dishwasher moment six months later!

TWITTER PHOTO SHARING

One of the things that we try to do with a social media campaign is move people from Community #3 (Ambient Fans) to Community #2 (Engaged Fans), and then to Community #1 (Super Fans). Posting photos to Twitter is a great way to do this.

It's easy to share a photo in a tweet. When you begin to compose a new tweet or an @, a little icon of a camera will pop up below your tweet. Click on it to take a photo with your computer or upload any photo from your hard drive, desktop, or camera roll. You can also take photos using your mobile, and post them directly to Facebook or to your Twitter stream.

Instagram - http://www.instagram.com

You may have read about the fact that Instagram was purchased for $1 billion by Facebook. So it's safe to say it's here to stay. It's fun because it super easy to use and makes editing and sharing photos a snap! Instagram has 15 different filter options and buttons to post directly to Twitter, Facebook, Flickr, Tumblr, Foursquare, or send them by email. Other Instagramers can follow users, "like" pictures, comment, and mark favorite images easily as well. The pictures don't show up directly in your Twitter stream, but they are one click away.

Twitpic & YFrog - http://www.twitpic.com & http://www.yfrog.com

These two, and many other apps and services, allow you to use your mobile phone to snap pictures and easily upload them to your Twitter account as links on your tweet stream. This will also show up on your Facebook if you have them connected.

E. YOUR TWITTER HOME PAGE

Here is how to navigate your Twitter home page (http://www.twitter.com), from left to right across the top.

1. Home - Tab

The "Home" icon will bring you back to your home page. This will bring you to your profile page on Twitter, which displays *only* your tweet stream, regardless of when you sent them. When people come to check out your Twitter page, this is what they see. Your stream gives visitors an idea of your personality, and the full scope of your Tweets is often used to determine whether or not they want to follow you (this is why you want to share quality tweets three times a day).

2. @ Connect – Click on this to see who's sending you @ messages here. *TIP: always respond to anyone who sends you an @ - its great practice!*

3. # Discover – The links and stories curated here are automatically chosen by Twitter, depending on your tastes (some are paid ads & article links)

4. Search Box – The grey search box at the upper right of your Twitter homepage can be used to search for words and phrases used in tweets. It's a great way to find other people discussing the topics you like, and you can follow them.

5. Profile Icon - Click the profile icon to the right of the search box on the top right of the home page. You will see the following in a drop-down list:

> **Direct Messages (DMs)** - All of your direct messages will be archived here (note: some will be spam). These are only visible to the recipient and sender of the message, and they are not posted publicly like a normal tweet or @reply.

NOTE: In order to send a DM the person MUST be following you and you must be following them back, otherwise it won't work.

6. To Compose a New Tweet

At the top, right-hand side of the screen, next to the search box and the Settings icon you will find a blue box. Click on it to compose a new tweet.

7. How to Create a Twitter List

From the dashboard on your Twitter home page, click the profile drop-down menu on the right-hand side. When you scroll down the menu, click "Lists."

On the right side of your screen you should see the button, "Create a List," where a pop-up box will appear prompting you to give a list name and a description. Note: You can either make this list public, so others have access to the list, or private, so only you can see this list.

Once you have created the list, you can either use the search box to find people to add to the list, or click on "following" so you can see a list of those Twitter users you follow to add to the list.

Next to each name of the person you are following, there is a drop-down menu that allows you to add or remove each person to a list. Click on the list to which you would like to add them. Remember, you can always add more Twitter lists later.

F. HOW TO BRAND/SKIN YOUR PAGE

The Black Keys (@theblackkeys) have excellent branding on their Twitter page. Their background matches their profile picture and they have a side-bar that allows fans to see the title of their newest album.

The branding is simple and succinct. As a musician, you are constantly competing with so many other bands for a fan's attention.

By branding your page properly, it will become much more memorable.

G. THE CYBER PR® GUIDE TO INCREASING TWITTER FOLLOWERS

Twitter is, in my humble opinion, the fastest way to grow your fan base. Here is a time tested strategy we have executed for multiple Cyber PR® clients. It takes some time and TLC, but it works!

To be safe, I do *not* recommend following more than 500 people every 24 hours, because if you are near 800 or 900, you could be flagged for "strange activity" (Twitter's phrase). Alternatively, if you follow between 100 - 300 new people each time, you should be okay, as far as steering clear of issues.

EIGHT STEPS TO GROWING MUTUAL FOLLOW-BACK RELATIONSHIPS

1. Think of an artist you like (who has similar fans to you).

2. Type in any band or solo artist that influences you in the search box on the top right-hand side of your Twitter home page.

3. Click on any profile with a decent number of followers. Once you get to that profile, click on the "followers" link on the top right hand side of their home page.

4. You will now see a long list of profiles that you could follow. (Move down the list and start following by clicking the grey follow box with the little Twitter bird on the right of each profile.) I highly suggest that you don't get too nitpicky and read every profile - unless one looks fishy, or there is no bio or photo. Just follow - you can always unfollow later.

5. Repeat this process for several minutes until you follow around 300 people.

6. Wait at least two to three days to give the people who you followed ample time to follow you back. During those two to three days, you will notice some of the people that you followed will reciprocate by following you back and you will have many new followers.

7. Until you have over 2,000 followers of your own, you only have the ability to follow up to 2,000 profiles at one time. Be sure to *unfollow* those who are NOT following you back. tweepi.com & manageflitter.com will help you swiftly identify and unfollow those who do not follow you back or who do not have profile pictures, etc.

8. After you have 2,000 followers, you will be able to follow more users, but that will be dependent on how many people are following you. So, after you break 2,000 people, it may be advantageous for you to only follow back the people who are very active.

ADDING TWITTER "FOLLOW ME" ICONS TO YOUR PAGES

People respond to Calls To Action online. So just having Twitter is a great start, but having a Twitter icon that says: "Follow me on Twitter" is a great invitation. Particularly, adding a Twitter icon that matches your look and feel is a very effective way to get more followers.

Here are a few places where you can find open-source Twitter icons to add to your Web pages:

100 GREAT TWITTER ICONS

Hongkiat is a site for designers and bloggers and they created a master list of 100 great Twitter icons easily laid out for you to see and choose from.

http://bit.ly/100TwitterIcons

NOT ENOUGH? HERE ARE 300 MORE!

Small Business CEO blog has a full directory of even more varied designs. They are all free as well.

http://smbceo.com

http://bit.ly/300TwitterIcons

ADDING TWEET STREAM TO YOUR WEBSITE AND SOCIAL MEDIA SITES

Adding your tweet stream so that it automatically feeds to your home page, blog, LinkedIn, and Facebook kills a lot of birds (no pun intended) with just a few keystrokes. This also guarantees your content will always stay fresh just by updating your Twitter.

You can find two great blog posts that have wonderful integration tools from Sitepoint and NetTuts. If you are unclear on how to add your tweet stream to your social media pages and website, any Web designer should be able to do it in just a few minutes: http://bit.ly/10TwitterIntegrations http://bit.ly/5TwitterIntegrations

ADDING A RETWEET BUTTON TO YOUR BLOG

I'm sure you have seen this if you have read any blogs recently. It's from the website http://addthis.com and it inserts a retweet button within each of your blog posts so you can easily share, and be shared, on Twitter.

H. MANAGING THE NOISE ON TWITTER:

CYBER PR®'S TOP TWITTER MANAGEMENT TOOL

There are dozens of tools that you can use to manage Twitter. However, in our humble opinion, you only need one: Hootsuite http://hootsuite.com

Hootsuite is the perfect app if you have multiple Twitter accounts that you want to manage. I also love the scheduling feature. You can program your tweets for marketing, Follow Friday #FF, Music Monday #MM, holiday or birthday tweets in advance by date and time – just set it and forget it! You can also monitor @ Mentions, RT's, and every time keywords and hashtags that matter to you get mentioned.

By scheduling some of your tweets and status messages, you can free up your time for other things (like practicing music!). 2 versions are available — Free and $8.99 per month (worth it for the analytics that they provide) .

Done! You have filtered out the noise and you are bringing Community #3 (Ambient Fans) closer to being your Communities #2 (Engaged Fans), and #1 (Super Fans).

I. CYBER PR®'S TOP MOBILE PHONE APPS FOR TWITTER

There are so many apps for mobile phones and you don't need a fancy-schmancy phone to support your Twitter updates. Again, we recommend HootSuite.

1. Hootsuite Mobile Apps

Hootsuite Mobile Apps come in three forms – iPhone, Android and Blackberry:

>http://hootsuite.com/iphone
>
>http://hootsuite.com/blackberry, @hootberry, @HootSuiteiPhone
>
>http://hootsuite.com/android, @hootdroid

2. The Great Standby: Plain Old Text – 40404

Yep, it's BASIC and it works! To text from your mobile phone from the USA, send messages to 40404 (make sure you set it up on your Twitter account first by entering your mobile number) and they will immediately go to your Twitter feed. To message friends who follow you from your mobile phone, you can type "d" (for direct) then their user- name. This is very useful when you are out and about and you don't have their mobile phone numbers.

J. CYBER PR®'S TOP APPS FOR SHARING MUSIC ON TWITTER

1. Spotify

You can easily share tracks, albums and whole and playlists using the share icon next to every track within Spotify. Simply add your own comment or hashtag and *voila!*

http://spotify.com, @spotify

2. Blip.fm

Blip is a music discovery site that allows users to cross-post their discoveries to Twitter. A blip is a combination of 1) a song and 2) a tweet.

Here is a great blog post by @SharonHayes from 2009 but still awesome today!

http://tinyurl.com/BlipBlog, http://blip.fm, @blipfm

3. Tweet For A Track

This app allows you to upload your song and post it to both Twitter and Facebook. If your fans retweet your message, they get your track free and you can track and keep their Twitter handles for fan base building. It's viral marketing through Twitter.

http://www.tweetforatrack.com, @tweetforatrack

4. #Music - Twitter's Music App

Twitter has recently made an effort to join the music discovery game by launching Twitter #Music (through their acquisition of the popular social music discovery website "We Are Hunted"). Unfortunately Twitter's effort has fallen short in regards to discovery for independent musicians, as their platform is a simple music chart, broken into two views - "popular" and "emerging." In both cases, Twitter Music's charts display artists, either "popular" (being streamed by a vast majority of users / aka signed to a Major Label) or "emerging" artists, based on how much engagement they are getting. If you have a Spotify or Rdio premium account you can listen to the entirety of the songs; if you have iTunes you get a 30-second clip and the option to buy.

In essence, Twitter #Music is no different than any other social media-focused Music Chart such as Billboard's Social 50 chart. At the time this book was published (spring 2013) the #Music app is still releasing new updates. It may be possible that Twitter will soon release an update for emerging artists.

K. MEASURING YOUR EFFECTIVENESS ON TWITTER

TWITTER ANALYTICS

So, now that we've taken you through the tactical points of Facebook and Twitter, and you're on a roll with your new-found knowledge, it's time to dig into something that is critical: Your Analytics.

Analytics are the key to understanding your marketing effectiveness and your fan base. When you learn how to use them well, they will show you what is working effectively versus what is not.

Once you can get a handle on these key differentiators in your analytics, you can do more of what works and less of what doesn't, to capture and engage more fans.

USE ANALYTICS TO SUPERCHARGE YOUR TWITTER BASE

STEP 1: Go to Your "Home" Page

Go to your home page on Twitter (press the "Home" tab next to the search box at the top of your profile). Your Timeline (stream) will be displayed.

STEP 2: Look at Your @ Mentions

Click on @Mentions tab - Scroll down your @ Mentions and see if certain people stand out (people who have responded more than two times or people you know). Make sure you are following everyone who @'s you.

STEP 3: Create a List

Create a list for these followers so you can monitor them. And make SURE to interact with them regularly. Call your list whatever you like. For example: "People I Love."

L. CYBER PR®'S TOP FIVE APPS FOR TRACKING TWITTER ANALYTICS

After you get a handle on this, for deeper engagement, here are a few Twitter analytics applications we suggest:

1. TweetStats - http://tweetstats.com

This site is AMAZING because it will help you get your tweets in balance. Simply enter your Twitter username and it graphs out for you everything you will need to know including:

- Who you retweet the most (and what % of your tweets are RT's)
- Who you @ the most (and what % of your tweets are @'s)
- What days and times you tend to tweet the most
- Your top five most used words!
- And more!

2. Twitter Counter - http://twittercounter.com

Twitter Counter is an app that shows you how many Twitter followers you have and it provides a graph of the growth of your followers over time that they deliver to your inbox via email once a week. It's a great tool to keep you aware of your effectiveness because it shows your current followers, your growth each week, and your prediction for next week.

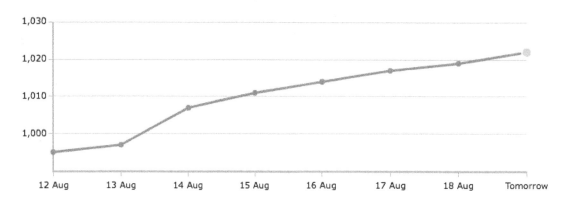

4. Tweet Reach - http://tweetreach.com

Tweet Reach shows many people saw your tweets and, more importantly, it identifies which of your followers have helped you get the most exposure. Each pie slice on their graphs show you how many people saw how many of your tweets and who they were. You can also run reports for your hashtags.

5. Twit Block - http://twitblock.org

Worried about spammers? Some people we talk to say that they have a rash of spammers who follow them and load their tweet streams with spam. If you have this problem, TwitBlock is an app that scans your followers for signs of "spamminess" making it easy and quick to block the unscrupulous ones in one hit.

6. Tweepi - http://tweepi.com

At $7.49 a month this service will help you get rid of unfollowers, clean up inactive accounts and follow new appropriate people.

M. FIVE TIPS FOR MUSICIANS FROM LAURA FITTON, CO-AUTHOR OF "TWITTER FOR DUMMIES"

Laura Fitton (@Pistachio) is one of the most well-known users of Twitter. I interviewed her to get her perspective on how musicians can use Twitter to grow their fan bases.

Laura: "The opportunity for musicians is huge. If an ordinary person like me can suddenly get an audience and a micro, mini-celebrity kind of thing going on, someone with a bona fide audience and something to consistently give their audience, like their music, can build something substantial using Twitter."

Tip #1: Twitter = Free Portable Marketing

"Twitter is portable. If you're on tour, you can use Twitter from a mobile base, like a cell phone or tablet. And it's quick. It's very hard for someone who's always on the go to sit down and blog, or really spend a lot of time in front of a computer trying to share content. But being able to do it through your mobile is really powerful and very cool.

Remember you are not just sharing text! Use links to share audio, photos, videos, live video streams off a cell phone and more. Imagine you're backstage at a gig warming up and you suddenly give your fans a little sneak preview into what that looks like."

Tip #2: It's Anti- In-Your-Face Communication

"A lot of what makes Twitter powerful is that it's not in-your-face business communication. It's not that "I want something from you... here's my business card," kind of transaction. It's very authentic. You're only remarking on stuff you would remark on out of the power of your own heart."

Tip #3: Use Twitter to Reveal Depth and Authenticity

"That depth and authenticity also means that you could go to a total stranger's Twitter page right now and read their last one to four pages of tweets - just little 140-character messages, links, comments, remarks, jokes and complaints. If you read four pages of that, which is about 80 little tweets in all, you'd get an amazingly accurate sense of what they're like. It's very hard to convince people that this is so, but the more I've interacted with people, the more I've discovered toral personalities on Twitter."

Tip #4 Keep in Mind: It's About Meeting Offline Too

"Incidentally, one big mistake people make is that they think it all happens online. The major friendships, business relationships and opportunities that have come to me have been like lasagna, different layers. Meeting online, meeting at a conference, hanging out online more, seeing each other at another event, building up a big kind of connected thing. But when I do meet the people in person, it's true that I know them pretty well, just from those little offhand remarks. And it always astonishes me."

Tip #5: You Need Critical Mass for it to Make Sense

"One of the first things I would say to any musician is, let's face it, you obviously don't write and perform music just so you can sell it and make money. You do it for emotional connection. You do it for deep personal expression. You do it because you want to change something in the world. You do it because you feel a certain way and you want other people to understand how you feel. Right?

All the basic motivating things that drive you to be a musician are the things that are going to make you really good at something like Twitter. Because Twitter isn't about push, push, push the music. Obviously, you want your music to sell in order to survive and be able to pour more into your art. But at the center of your art, the work you've put in, the talent you've acquired, the things you know about music, the things you're trying to figure out in your lyrics or in your performances, these are the soulful aspects of what you do and why.

This sounds silly when I talk to executives, believe me. But for musicians, it's great because all those soulful things are going to make you successful on Twitter. People want personality. They want authenticity. They want a genuine look at the person behind the music.

Then, when you do have a new album, when you do have a signing party, when you do have a tour going on, you can let your fans know in a way that gets them excited about telling other people and advocating for you... because you've spent most of your time engaging with them as humans."

N. PEOPLE TO FOLLOW ON TWITTER

OUR TOP CHOICES TO FOLLOW ON TWITTER:

@allmyfriendsmag
@allmusic
@altpress
@aquadrunkard
@artistdata
@artistshouse
@ascap
@bandcamp
@bandzoogle
@berkleemusic
@bigchampagne
@bmi
@bobbyowsinski
@caricole
@cashmusic
@cdbaby
@citybeatcincy
@contactmusic
@coslive
@cyberpr
@dave_cool
@earmilkdotcom
@future_of_music
@glidemag
@hellomusic
@hostbaby
@hypebot
@iancrogers
@independentrock
@indie_musiccom
@indieambassador
@indiemusicrev
@lrrmusic
@kbylin
@knowthemusicbiz
@lefsetz
@madalynsklar
@makeitinmusic
@marteeeen
@miccontrol
@michaelsb
@mountflorida
@mrbuzzfactor
@music_nomad
@musicdish
@musicmuso
@musicsuccessin9
@musicthinktank
@muzikman
@narmmusic
@nextbigsound
@nimbit
@nme
@northerntrans
@nprmusic
@orchtweets
@pitchforkmedia
@pledgemusic
@plugola
@ReverbNation
@rockethub
@rootmusic
@sesac
@sivers
@songtrust
@sonicbids
@sonicbidspanos
@soundexchange
@soundopinions
@sputnikmusic
@stereogum
@theprp
@thornybleeder
@topspinmedia
@valleyarm
@verbicide
@wearelistening

MUSIC INDUSTRY THOUGHT LEADERS:

@dubber
@futurehitdna
@future_of_music
@hypebot
@MrBuzzFactor
@sivers
@MicControl
@CBracco
@DannyDee

@rynda	@ArtistData	@CrowdSurf
@ReverbNation	@fanbridge	@Nimbit
@RocketHub	@PledgeMusic	@marcuswhitney

WEB THOUGHT LEADERS & BRILLIANT MARKETING PEEPS:

@chrisbrogan	@briansolis	@davedelaney
@cspenn	@leelefever	@stevegarfield
@charleneli	@Ed_Dale	@jeffpulver
@jowyang	@jasonvo	@sethgodin

O. CONNECTING FACEBOOK & TWITTER

While there are a lot of strategies that will allow you to cut down on the amount of content you'll need to create, as well as the amount of time spent using social media, connecting Facebook and Twitter is one you want to avoid.

Connecting Facebook and Twitter is not a two-way, time saving opportunity. Your Facebook can very easily be connected to your Twitter account because the text component of your Facebook posts will very easily translate into Tweets. However, Twitter should never be connected back to Facebook (so that your tweets show on your Facebook Fan Page) for two very important reasons. The first is that the optimal number of Facebook posts per day is one. With Twitter however, you are really free to post as often as you'd like - if your tweets are posting to Facebook, you will be WAY over-publishing to your Fan Page. The second reason is that Facebook is all about multimedia. Photos, videos and links are far more likely to be engaged with on Facebook than simple text post. It is quite likely that your Tweets will lack engagement when republished to Facebook and should be avoided.

WORD TO THE WISE

Quite a few studies have shown that a Facebook Fan Page is most effective when only posted on once or twice a day. So, while you can now combine your Facebook and Twitter accounts effectively (a HUGE time-saver for the busy, independent artist), you want to be careful not to over post to your Facebook Fan Page from Twitter.

If you already have your Twitter and Facebook accounts linked, you may want to un-link them and re-link them so that you get all the new features.

INSTRUCTIONS FOR INSTALLING TWITTER ON YOUR FAN PAGE

1. Go to the top bar across the top of your Twitter home page and look for the icon of the person (it's in between the search box and the blue "compose new tweet"). A drop down box is associated with this icon that says "Settings."

2. Under the "Profile" section on the left sidebar, scroll down and you should see a box that says Facebook - post tweets to Facebook.

3. If you do not see it - login to Facebook and search for Twitter - click on the first Twitter Icon that pops up - it will prompt you to login to Twitter.

It looks like this:

4. Click the yellow button and then look at the twitter settings again. The Facebook icon should show up

5. Click it and it should begin to install.

6. In order to see your Fan Page, click the tiny check box to the left of the words of my Facebook page and pull the page you want from the drop down box (if you administer more than one Fan Page there will be several here)

7. Select the page you want associated with this account.

8. Click on blue "save changes" box!

Voila! You have connected your Personal Page to your Fan Page.

P. ARIEL'S SOUND TAKEAWAYS

- Branding your profile is crucial—make sure you have a photo, bio, links and a background skin that matches who you are online—just choosing a default twitter background won't cut it

- Understanding the basics will change your life on Twitter (@, RT, DM & Hashtags)

- It is virtually impossible to over tweet—six times a day is recommended

- Mix it up—make sure you are tweeting photos, music, videos and articles as well as retweeting and @ replying people

- Share links using bit.ly—it's a great way to shorten long links and you can track your results

- Your Lists are key! Group great people together and make sure to interact

- Analyze your Twitter account often, and interact with your strongest followers (the ones who have the most followers and tweet most often)

CHAPTER 4: *YouTube*

A. ROOM THREE IN YOUR SOCIAL MEDIA HOUSE

YouTube Stats You Need to Know

- It is the second largest search engine (bigger than Bing, Yahoo, ASK, and Yahoo all combined)

- More than one billion unique users visit YouTube every month

- Four billion hours of video are viewed on YouTube every month

- Every second, there are nearly 50,000 YouTube videos being viewed all around the world

- 72 hours of video are uploaded every minute, resulting in nearly twelve years of content uploaded every day

- More than 50 percent of videos on YouTube have been rated or include comments from the YouTube community

- YouTube is a social network, not just a video site

YouTube is a critical social media site to include in your arsenal of social media/online marketing techniques. There is no way to refute the power of video, or of the site: YouTube is the second largest online search engine. It has hundreds of millions of users from around the world and is localized in 53 countries across 61 languages.

In 2006, Google bought YouTube for $1.65 billion dollars. So, YouTube now operates as a subsidiary of Google (which is, of course, the largest online search engine). It's important to understand how they relate to each other in order to maximize your presence.

YouTube is an interactive social network just like Facebook or Twitter, and you are encouraged to make friends with other users. I'm often shocked that artists expect to simply post a video on YouTube, make no friends on the site, watch no one else's videos and still "go viral." Making friends, leaving comments, and "thumbing up" as many videos as you can are key moves on the YouTube platform.

If you start looking around online, you will see people leading you back to their YouTube channels all over the Internet. If you see links to YouTube on people's Facebook, Twitter, websites, or blogs: head on over, subscribe to their channels, watch videos, leave comments, and make friends. That's how to be social!

TIP: Being active on YouTube is a great newsletter-building strategy. Once you engage someone on YouTube and get into a conversation with them, you can ask if you can add them to your newsletter.

FIVE COMPELLING REASONS TO USE YOUTUBE

1. Market yourself and your music on the world's second-largest search engine.

2. Interact with fans, music professionals and other artists.

3. Create videos that appear in Google search results. Be Google-icious!

4. Attract more fans.

5. Become a viral sensation!

EIGHT YOUTUBE BEST PRACTICES:

1. Watch What is Already Working, and Follow!

Before you upload a well-produced video of yourself performing or pay for a multi-million dollar camera shoot, I strongly caution you to take a look at what is "going viral" on YouTube. They make this easy by posting the current most-viewed videos here: http://www.youtube.com/charts. I suggest you watch the most viewed videos in the music categories for several weeks, and see if you can decipher a trend or come up with an idea that might fit on this most-viewed chart list before you outline your own content strategy or add to it.

2. Think about Your Audience

Keep in mind who your audience is, and where they watch. Many people watch videos while they are at work. And people pass along videos that are funny, amusing, or interesting to them in some form or fashion.

3. Make Your Video Less Than Three Minutes

Why? We live in a short-attention-span world, and anything longer will reduce your chance of the entire video being watched.

4. Always Include a Call to Action

Remember, in order to get people to take action, you need to tell them what to do. Add a Call to Action (CTA) to every video you post. A CTA could be "Follow us on Twitter," "Like us on Facebook," or "Visit Our Site." Only include one CTA in each video you post so you don't confuse your audience. Without a CTA, you are leaving potential traffic on the table. The whole point of videos is to drive traffic back to your site. (You remember that, yes?)

5. It Doesn't Have to be Fancy or Expensive to Go Viral!

Look at the charts. There are a lot of videos on YouTube that are lo-fi, not "produced," and they get millions of views.

6. Remember the Purpose of Videos

It is important to remember the reason you make videos in the first place! It is not just about getting a lot of views (that's just the beginning); it is to get people to take an action. Whether that action is coming back to your website or following you on Facebook or Twitter, it's critical to remember why you made your video. Keep your eye on the end goal and make sure you constantly measure your videos' effectiveness.

7. Know What People are Searching for

Caution: YouTube is a search engine. This means people are searching for things that they already know and love on YouTube. So, including content that people already know is crucial, because they are already looking for it! Here is a site (set up by YouTube) where you can actually research exactly what people are searching for, word for word: https://ads.youtube.com/keyword_tool

COVER SONGS REALLY WORK!

A few months ago, I interviewed YouTube cover song phenomenon Tiffany Alvord. She explained her formula for how she got millions of viewers to watch her videos: http://bit.ly/ViralVidTiffany

There was quite a reaction to this interview. I was met with a lot of sneering, older musicians saying, "I'm not a hot, young teen. I can't do that." If you are having this same reaction, my answer to you is, "Yes, you can!"

Granted, there is a trend on YouTube of many young teens creating videos of cover songs from their bedrooms. And some of these videos garner millions of views. However, talented grownups can do this too!

On the next page is an example of a Cyber PR® artist, Jane Lui, who uses covers beautifully to attract fans (and she is well above 16!):

http://www.youtube.com/LuieLand

Before you start writing off this strategy as something for tweens; think again. Fans that already know and love many songs that are near and dear to their hearts may actually find out about you if you create a cover song that captivates them!

B. SET UP YOUR OWN YOUTUBE CHANNEL IN FIVE STEPS

It's easy to set up your very own channel at YouTube. Just go to http://youtube.com and press the big button on the top of the page that says "Create Account." You can then choose a username for your channel. If you have a Gmail account (because, again, Google owns YouTube), it will assign your Gmail username as your channel name, and then you can edit it.

1. Be Consistent Across Platforms

Make sure your channel name matches your website and your username on Facebook and Twitter. Ideally, you should make your user name your band's/artist's name. If that name is unavailable, add something like "music" or "official" onto your user name.

2. Your Channel Name Should Include Keywords

Remember, YouTube is owned by Google, and keywords are very important. So, if you are not using your artist name, think about which keywords fit you and your music.

3. Choose Musician Channel

Login and go to your page. Click on the "Settings" tab at the top of the page and select "Musician" as the channel type.

4. Choose Your Themes and Colors

Next to "Settings" you will see the "Channel Design" tab. Here you can choose different colors, upload a background image, and select your text and hyperlink colors.

TIP #1: Make sure your colors match your overall branding: your website, blog, Facebook account, Twitter account.

TIP #2: It's very hard to read darkly-colored fonts against a black background. Choose colors that are easy on the eyes for the sake of your visitors. And remember, white is never a bad choice.

5. Upload Your Videos

Go to the "My Videos and Playlists" tab and click on the blue button on the top left that says "New." Select "video upload" and start adding your videos.

C. OPTIMIZING YOUR CHANNEL

1. Titles are Key

I've been reading a lot of YouTube studies, and it turns out that the single biggest contributing factor to your success on a video click through will be directly related to how you title your video.

TIP #1: Make sure that the title of each of your videos includes your artist or band name, song title, and any other relevant information.

TIP #2: If it's not a straight-ahead music video, create a title that will make the viewer want to watch the video. Something captivating and catchy is key. (However, remember that it must relate back to the actual video.)

2. The Description Box is Crucial

The description box is critical to optimization of your channel. Always start with your URL at the very beginning of the description box and don't forget to include http:// or else it will not show up as a hyperlink. And it's not a bad idea to add this link (or a link to your Facebook, Twitter, etc. at the end of the description as well).

3. Select a Proper Video Category

This will more than likely be "music." But it could be "humor" or "education" too. Remember to think about which best fits your content!

4. Tag Thoroughly

Google ranks tags, so always start with the tag that is the most important. If you are adding a title that is more than one word, put it in quotes—i.e., "Sympathy For The Devil"—or else the words will become individual tags. Don't overdo the number of tags. (Google frowns upon over-tagging, so keep it to seven or eight at the most). Some tag ideas: artist/band name, song name, any related artists names (especially if you add a cover), similar artists (so that when people type in an artist they like, they will come across your video), genres of music, hometown, names of all band members, producer, themes in video, etc.

TIP: Don't overdo it! Your build-out will take some time. YouTube moderates user activity closely, much as Facebook moderates its own user activity. If you receive a notice to stop sending messages, adding friends, and so on, STOP, or else your account will be deleted. And you don't want that!

5. Subscribe to Other Channels

Subscribing to other channels can help you go a long way. Search for keywords that match yours. Start by subscribing to channels of similar artists or artists that influenced you or that you sound like. After you have subscribed to your favorite artist's channels, start subscribing to their fans' channels by going to the artist's channel and locating the "Subscribers" box. This will be a good place to start adding friends.

6. Add Videos as Favorites

Love a video on YouTube? Just click on the little heart. Keep in mind that these videos will be added to your "Favorites" section on your channel.

7. Comment on Videos

Respond to other people's comments, just as you would respond to others' comments on Facebook.

8. Rate the Comments

You can click on the "thumbs up" or "thumbs down." This process takes only about one second per rating.

D. TIPS FROM A YOUTUBE INSIDER

Ryan Carey (@ryanwcarey) worked at Youtube for 5 years and is now a freelance video strategist and media trainer based in San Francisco and Brooklyn. The following are Ryan's 6 pieces of advice on building a personal brand through video:

1. Your videos are not going to go viral

I'm sorry. The news had to be broken. The closest word in our English language to 'viral' is miracle. Now that our dreams have been crushed, it's time we begin putting in work to be serious (and taken seriously) with video.

2. Take time building a home

This is the difference between straw and brick. Do you have a YouTube 'account' (it's called a channel)? Did you sign up and never put anything more into it? If yes, you have a YouTube house made of straw. One needs to take time setting up a channel properly, learn basic editing and be able to offer consistent polished content. This is what I call YouTube muscle – which means investing some sweat in building the brick foundation. Once complete, maintenance is lowered (still very relevant) and you can focus more on your content.

3. If it's not fun, you're doing it wrong

As a culture, we have gone from sitting in front of the TV watching a total of 5 channels to having power at our fingertips to create any style of show we want. We can assume the role of stars and no one has to approve it or give us a deal. If someone had come 30 years ago and said we'd someday be able to make our own shows, we'd all be excited. That is fun.

4. We are all making shows

This might be your first season. How many episodes will you make? How long will they be? What's yours about? How often will you release them? Reading this may seem overwhelming, but it's not. It's just work that goes into building the muscle to make your personal brand smoother on video.

5. Polish

This is the difference between showing up to a black tie affair in jeans versus a tuxedo. Polish means a concise video, an accurate description, your own intro/outro and smooth transitions every single time. It also means asking yourself if the audience will stay engaged with what you've made. If you answer no, tighten it up and tuck in your shirt.

6. Don't waste time

Both yours and the audience's. Everyone knows attention spans are at an all time low. YouTube is no different. If your video doesn't pop until 25 seconds in, you may lose half the viewers. If there is a 3 second pause of you thinking on camera about what you're going to say, that's a risk of releasing the audience member who could easily become a lifetime fan loyal to your personal brand. Or at the very least a subscriber.

Be fast. Be loud. Be confident.

You're not a sitcom nor a reality show. You get to choose who you are on camera, and whoever you choose, ensure it's professional.

E. YOUTUBE MARKETING IDEAS

SHARE VIDEO ON SOCIAL MEDIA SITES: TWITTER, FACEBOOK & BLOG

One of the best parts of YouTube is that it's easy to share videos using the embed codes and share buttons that YouTube provides. And a solid marketing strategy involves cross posting your videos on your site, on your blog, and on your social media sites. According to YouTube, a link to your video in a tweet "results in six new YouTube.com sessions on average." So, once you post your videos on YouTube, post them on Twitter as well!

LEAVE A VIDEO RESPONSE

You are on a video channel. How about leaving a video in the comments section instead of just leaving a written response? If you see a cover song getting thousands (or millions) of views, leave your OWN version of the song right there on the page. However, be careful! We call this "putting yourself in harm's way." We call it this because the video has the potential to backfire. People might be annoyed with it and leave negative comments, but there is still the potential to reach people and get more fans.

HOW TO LEAVE A VIDEO RESPONSE

STEP 1: Find a video you like.

STEP 2: Click on "Leave Video Response" under the comments section.

STEP 3: Depending on whether you have a video already created, or you want to create a video on the spot, click "Upload Video" or "Create Video."

STEP 4: Post your video! Tell them why you love their video/channel, or whatever else you're thinking. The more you interact, the better!

TRACK YOUR EFFECTIVENESS WITH "INSIGHT"

When you are logged into your channel you will see a tab on the top called "Insight." Click on it to take a deep dive into your analytics. Here you will be able to see all demographics of your viewers—male or female, where they live, etc.—and on which days your videos got the most views. You can also track where the views are coming from, which is key to determining your future marketing strategies. Looking at "Insight" will also allow you to see if your CTAs (Calls to Action) are working.

ADD YOUR EVENTS

You can also add your shows under the "New" button. It's a great idea to sync your shows here for extra promotional "oomph!"

By mastering the tips in this chapter and following the YouTube strategies outlined in this book, you will be head and shoulders above a vast majority of artists who use the site without any guidance.

F. FIVE EXAMPLES OF GREAT ARTIST CHANNELS

1. Pomplamoose - http://www.youtube.com/user/pomplamoosemusic

The YouTube sensation Pomplamoose is comprised of Jack Conte and Nataly Dawn. They started posting videos in 2008, and are known for their quirky re-harmonization of pop songs such as Beyonce's "Single Ladies" and Lady Gaga's "Telephone." They play all instruments on the tracks and create videos that go back and forth between the artists playing and singing. Their quirk and charm have gotten them millions of views!

How They Did It: They did this by capitalizing on the searches fans were performing on the already existing Billboard Charting songs. Then, they capitalized on the hits generated.

2. Mac Miller - http://www.youtube.com/user/TreeJTV

Through a strong YouTube presence, Mac Miller went, in a few short years, from teenage hip-hop artist based out of Pittsburgh, to becoming the first independent artist to have the #1 selling album on the Billboard chart.

How He Did It: With a steady flow of new music being released through multiple mixtapes, artist features/collaborations, EPs and a full-length LP, Mac Miller released several, low-budget, yet incredibly high-quality music videos to accompany each project. Through this strategy, Mac Miller was almost consistently featured on blogs, allowing him to build up an incredibly dedicated fan base on other social platforms such as Facebook and Twitter.

3. Rebecca Black - http://www.youtube.com/user/rebecca

Rebecca's mother paid $4,000 to Ark Music Factory (A music house known for cranking out young, bubble-gum pop videos) for her video "Friday" and there was an instant response. Rebecca has since been on Glee, Good Morning America, and more.

How She Did It: This went viral, but the overwhelming response was *not* at all positive. Many dubbed it as "the worst song and music video ever." There is a sad part of this story: on ABC's Nightline, Black revealed that she was forced to quit middle school because of real-world harassment and bullying. This makes me wonder, is the price of fame for a 13-year-old worth it when it comes to this?

4. Walk Off the Earth - http://www.youtube.com/user/walkofftheearth

This Canadian-based group racked up hundreds of millions of YouTube views with their Gotye cover, "Somebody I Used to Know." The band mixes popular cover songs (again benefitting from people searching for the songs on YouTube and Google) with original tunes and has gained a massive following with their innovative videos.

How They Did It: In their rendition, all five members huddled around one acoustic guitar (all playing on different parts of the instrument). This was so cool that it went viral. They had the innovation and talent to back it up.

5. Gotye - http://www.youtube.com/user/gotyemusic

Not only does this Belgian-Australian musician write amazing songs, Gotye's haunting songwriting, Sting-sounding voice, and avante garde music videos make him a unique artist at his age.

How He Did It: As Seth Godin says, artists have to be "remarkable," and Gotye has done just that; become someone people want to respond and "remark" about. He writes songs that everyone on YouTube wants to cover!

THREE MORE GREAT ARTIST CHANNELS TO CHECK OUT

We like these channels because their brand is clear and they are well designed. Take a look at them and see for yourself:

1. The Black Keys http://www.youtube.com/user/theblackkeys

2. Billboard Magazine http://www.youtube.com/user/BillboardMagazine

3. Portugal the Man http://www.youtube.com/user/Portugalthemanband

G. THE OFFICIAL YOUTUBE PLAYBOOK FOR MUSICIANS

YouTube has just launched a new series of "Playbooks" for content creators. There are several topics covered, and one of them is specifically written for musicians. This free eBook details strategies and best practices on how to build your music channel, and includes techniques to help guide success of your videos. Chapter themes are:

better optimization, how to release an album or song, content frequency, and how to effectively engage with your fans. It's downloadable on YouTube's website, and is a great resource for anyone looking to grow their audience on this platform.

Grab The Guide Here: http://bit.ly/YouTubeMusicianPlaybook

H. ARIEL'S SOUND TAKEAWAYS

- Make sure that your channel is skinned to match your branding, and all of your links and bio are visible and clear

- In order to have a successful YouTube presence, you must post videos often

- YouTube is a social network, and two-way engagement and following others is key

- Just having an official music video and some live tracks probably won't cause you to have much of a following

- Study what going viral really means by studying the types of videos that have already gone viral

- Understand how to select proper video categories and thoroughly tag each of your videos, so that you can be found

- Always include a clear call to action in each video you post

- Don't be obsessed with big numbers; small numbers can be wonderful. Do not ever buy views - it's just not worth it.

CHAPTER 5: *Blogging*

A. ROOM FOUR IN YOUR SOCIAL MEDIA HOUSE

Blog-tastic Facts

- There are literally over a 180 million blogs worldwide: with 64 million of those blogs made on WordPress and 50 million on Tumblr

- About 30 percent of bloggers consider blogging a full-time job

- Most bloggers are female

- The top five topics to blog about are technology, educational information, social media, fashion, and travel & leisure

- Every month, about three million new blogs appear on the Web

- The blogosphere is dominated by 25- to 44-year-olds

Blogging is a crucial piece of your social media strategy. Blogging also allows your fans to see more of you. However, it takes dedication and consistency to pull off a blogging strategy.

I believe that getting reviewed on blogs is critical for every musician because it helps create a bigger footprint for you online, builds awareness, and allows for a two-way conversation around your music.

All content on blogs is archived in Google and it can be a great portal for people to discover you when you blog consistently.

MOVIE TIME!

Here are two movies to help you wrap your mind around blogging:

> **RSS:** http://www.commoncraft.com/rss_plain_english

> **Blogs:** http://www.commoncraft.com/blogs

B. HOW TO MANAGE BLOG READING

Setting up your RSS reader is the perfect way to get the information you want (not only from blogs, but also from other sites you frequently visit) to come to you, instead of having to check constantly to see what has been updated.

1. Create Your Blog Reader Profile

Blog reader profiles are wonderful because they will show the blogger and the reader community that you have visited a blog even if you do not choose to comment each and every time. This leaves a trail of cyber breadcrumbs back to you, which shows others what you are interested in and where you have been.

So, if you visit a blog that has Gravatar installed, a photo of you/your band logo will show up on the blog you visited. This is a great way of becoming extra memorable to bloggers. http://en.gravatar.com

2. Dive In

According to the most recent statistics, there are currently over 180 million active bloggers. Some of these blogs are read by a few dozen people, but others are read by millions. And, as you likely know, blogs can be about any topic. The vast majority of bloggers create blogs for no financial gain whatsoever; in fact, it usually costs music bloggers money to host their files and maintain their blogs. A blog is usually a personal endeavor. Most bloggers create their blogs as an outlet where they can talk about things they are passionate about in their lives, their opinions, and the things that they like and dislike. A blog is basically an online diary.

Finding blogs that are right for you won't take long. Just dive in and start reading them. The ones that resonate will jump out at you.

C. HOW TO GET REVIEWED ON BLOGS

There are three ways to get into the blogging world (blogosphere), some requiring a little less time or technology than others:

1. Read blogs regularly and make comments on them often.

2. Read blogs, comment a lot, AND become a blogger!

3. Attend conferences and meet bloggers face to face.

I highly recommend that you get familiar with the blogging world by reading blogs, and contributing by leaving comments on blogs you like, about something the blogger wrote. Commenting on blogs is a very effective way to get known in the social media world. Commenting can also get you seen by bloggers that could potentially write about you and your music in the future. Include your signature file under your name and type out the name of your band with a link to either your website, Facebook Fan Page, or Twitter page. This is a subtle way of letting the blogger know you're a musician without saying, "Hey, review me!" If the blogger likes your observations about what they wrote, they may just review you.

As a recovered traditional publicist with a background in writing press releases, announcing things, and blatantly pitching my clients, I had to start from scratch and relearn everything I thought I knew about how to promote music when I started to approach bloggers.

Bloggers are a quirky lot. I know this because I've spent the last several years observing bloggers, interacting with bloggers through my business, and attending some of the most notable blog conferences on Earth.

So, how on Earth are you supposed to interrupt and say, "Hey blogger, come write about me in your personal diary?"

OPTION #1: START YOUR OWN BLOG

The #1 piece of advice you should follow if you're trying to get known in the blogosphere is "do as they do." Start your own blog. This is a good idea for many reasons, aside from attracting other bloggers. If you don't know the big secret already: bloggers read other bloggers' blogs! And with easy platforms like Tumblr, it's easier than ever before.

Even if you opt not to start your own blog, you need to know that having your own blog has many benefits for you as an artist.

D. TOP SEVEN REASONS EVERY MUSICIAN SHOULD BLOG

1. Blogging is a fabulous way of keeping your fans connected to you.

Blogging goes much deeper than 140 characters on Twitter or images on Flickr. Blogging also gives your fans a platform to have an in-depth, two-way conversations with you for the whole world to see.

2. Google loves blogs.

If you set your blog up properly, you'll be indexed on Google for anything and everything you write about. This means that people who were searching for other topics can find you. For instance, let's say you blog about your dog. A person who is searching for "yellow lab" could come across your blog entry, discover your music, and become a fan!

3. Blogging puts you on a level playing field with other bloggers.

Bloggers read other blogs, especially those pertaining to subjects they write about—like music. And a music blogger will trust you much more if you understand the whole world of blogging.

4. A blog allows you to invite your fans backstage and into your life so that they can see all sides of you... but only the sides you want to be seen. You are in control of your content. Fans can subscribe to your blog using an RSS reader and get new updates sent directly to them without having to visit your site over and over to check for new posts.

5. You can syndicate your blog posts all over the Internet.

ReverbNation, Facebook, Twitter, and your own website are just a few places where your blog posts can show up so people can see them and engage with you.

6. Starting a blogroll adds to your credibility with other bloggers.

Add bloggers who acknowledge your blog onto your blogroll, which is a list of links to the other blogs you like or recommend. This is usually placed in the sidebar of your blog. In the blog world, it's critical to associate your-self with other blogs and communities of people with whom you would like to connect and with bloggers and communities that want to connect with you.

7. Blogging gets you community feedback fast.

Not sure about a song lyric, a photo shoot, which night to have a gig? Ask your fans to weigh in with their opinions!

You don't have to only blog about your music; you can talk about your home life, your TV habits, your favorite foods, your day job, your fitness routine—anything! The key here is that you must post regularly and consistently. If you are in a band, having each band member contribute one post a month is a great way to keep new content flowing.

TIP: Don't overthink. Just post! Do not treat this like a show or think you have to make every sentence perfect. The point of a blog is that it is an informal endeavor. Just get posting, don't stress about it, and tweak it to death (I would, however, recommend spell check).

E. HOW TO SET UP A BLOG

I'm not going to go into the details about how to set them up because you can easily find guides on how to do this via Google.

However, the following sites are wonderful. And you can get going on them within minutes of signing up.

Blogger - http://www.blogger.com

WordPress - http://www.wordpress.com

Tumblr - http://www.tumblr.com

HostBaby - http://www.hostbaby.com

Bandzoogle - http://www.bandzoogle.com

For a more advanced approach to blogging, I would suggest hiring a Web designer to install a WordPress blog right onto your website. This should not cost you more than a few hundred dollars, and your blog will then be integrated into your site. I also suggest that you add "/blog" to your personal URL. For example, my blog can be found at www.CyberPRMusic.com/blog.

TIP: If you have a website hosted by HostBaby, they will set up your WordPress blog for you. Contact hostbaby@hostbaby.com. I highly suggest this route, because then your blog will be in the same place as your website and not on a Blogger or WordPress site. (And I also strongly advise you to build your website using the WordPress platform.)

OPTION #2: BECOME AN AVID BLOG READER AND COMMENT BACK

Option #2 is a bit less time consuming because you will not have to build and maintain your own blog, but you will still have to create personal relationships with bloggers. If you are going to go this route, I suggest you build a links page on your website, or become friends with bloggers on

Facebook and feature them in your top friends. You must acknowledge other blogs so that you are still somewhat in the two-way conversation, which is critical.

F. YOUR 10-20 BLOG TARGETS

IDENTIFY 10-20 BLOG TARGETS WHERE YOU WANT TO BE REVIEWED

Once you have your own blog up and running (if you are intimidated by this part, skip it; you can still get results), the next step is to identify in which blogs you would like to be included...and then start reading them and posting comments on them.

If you don't know how to search for blogs, here is a way to get started. Search blogs using these search engines:

Google Blog Search - http://www.blogsearch.google.com

Technorati - http://www.technorati.com

Hype Machine - http://hypem.com

Include your list of 10-20 target blogs in your blogroll. Some of the blogs you will likely find in your search are more widely read, like Pitchfork and Brooklyn Vegan. These are great targets, but I suggest you target blogs that are more likely to cover you based on what they are already writing about. Some of the most popular music blogs are indie rock centric, so if you don't play indie rock, you may not have a chance of getting included.

Search and see if any blog has already written about you. With 200 million blogs out there, it's possible you've been mentioned somewhere! If you find a post that mentions you, perfect! Post a comment back thanking them for their post and say something about their blog. The idea is to create a two-way conversation by talking about them. Use a signature file identifying yourself so they know where to visit you online.

Here's what my email signature file looks like:

> **Ariel Hyatt**
> **CYBER PR**®
> Digital Music Campaigns &
> Social Media Strategies for Musicians
> ariel@cyberprmusic.com
> http://www.cyberprmusic.com/blog
> http://www.twitter.com/cyberpr

AGAIN, I CANNOT STRESS THIS ENOUGH:

Your comments should never be self-promotional—not at first. They need to be about the blog, its content and/or the blogger. Comment on how you like their blog. Add feedback. Disagree or agree, but the key is participate.

When you're a blogger, you live for comments. It shows people are engaged by what you are writing. And for a blogger, this is critical.

TIP: Don't ask for a review on your first contact with a blogger—just make an observation about them and comment on what they are writing. There will be plenty of time to make yourself known later—this is a process that takes some time.

Don't forget that bloggers are people too, and all PR is about connecting personally. If you do not handle this tactfully, the blogger will sense that you are just trying to get something.

OPTION #3: ATTEND CONFERENCES & MEET BLOGGERS FACE-TO-FACE

This is a great way to get into the blogging community. Here are a few I suggest:

> **SXSW Interactive** - http://www.sxsw.com
> Mid-March in Austin, Texas

BlogHer - http://www.blogher.com/conferences
August in San Diego, California

BlogWorld & .com - http://www.blogworldexpo.com
November in Los Angeles, California

Can't travel? That's okay. There are tons of bloggers meeting up for drinks in every city and state in the U.S. and abroad, so log in and join a group. I randomly joined the podcasting NYC group and out of it have met some of my closest allies in the business. Meetups are highly recommended:

Meetup - http://www.meetup.com

G. THE CYBER PR® GUIDE TO FINDING BLOGS

BLOGS THAT COVER MUSIC

The Hype Machine - http://hypem.com

The Hype Machine is a network of music bloggers that, according to them: "keeps track of what music bloggers write about. We handpick a set of Kick-A music blogs and then present what they discuss for easy analysis, consumption, and discovery. This way, your odds of stumbling into awesome music or awesome blogs are high. This site also tracks the most blogged about artists and songs on their network. So log on and start finding bloggers you like!

MUSIC BUSINESS BLOGS

Cyber PR® - http://www.cyberprmusic.com/blog

Every week my team and I write about marketing and PR, interview new media makers, and review killer apps for musicians.

Hypebot - http://www.hypebot.com

A journal of music, technology, and the new music business.

Music Think Tank - http://www.musicthinktank.com

A group blog, bringing together key thinkers in the realm of online music business. (Disclaimer – I write for this blog.)

Derek Sivers - http://sivers.org/blog

Daily thoughts for entrepreneurs and musicians.

Artists House - http://www.artistshousemusic.org

Video interviews with top music industry professionals on a broad range of topics about music and music business.

CD Baby - http://www.diymusician.cdbaby.com

CD Baby's DIY Musician is a daily blog that focuses on digital music promotion advice.

Bandzoogle - http://www.bandzoogle.com/blog

The Bandzoogle blog offers weekly music promotion and artist website optimization advice.

Billboard - http://www.billboard.biz

One of the largest sites covering all aspects of the music industry.

Bobby Owsinski - http://www.music3point0.blogspot.com

Daily digital promotion, social media, and apps and tools from one of the most versatile and impressive music production writers.

SOCIAL MEDIA BLOGS

Mashable - http://www.mashable.com

Comprehensive reporting on any and all social media developments.

Brian Solis - http://www.briansolis.com

Brian Solis is globally recognized as one of the most prominent thought leaders and published authors in new media. A digital analyst, sociologist, and futurist, he has studied and influenced the effects of emerging media on business, marketing, publishing, and culture.

Seth Godin - http://sethgodin.typepad.com

Seth Godin is the Godfather of marketing. He has written 14 books and every single one has been a bestseller. His blog posts are simple and easy to digest on a daily basis and written in plain English. I recently interviewed him. Watch Seth and me in action:

What Seth Godin Can Teach the Music Industry

Part 1: http://bit.ly/ArielSeth1

Part 2: http://bit.ly/ArielSeth2

H. MEASURING THE EFFECTIVENESS OF YOUR BLOG WITH GOOGLE ANALYTICS

If you are using WordPress, there is a very simple way to add Google Analytics (GA) to your site without having to edit any code: Install a Google Analytics plugin to your blog!

What's a plugin? It's a software component that adds to the functionality of WordPress. This component "plugs into" the application.

You can find plugins here: http://bit.ly/google-analytics-smh

Note: Always make sure that the plugins you select are tested to be compatible with the version of WordPress you're using!

ADDING HTML CODE TO YOUR BLOG TEMPLATE

There is another way to add the analytics code to your site, which is more permanent, and slightly more involved. The code can be added into the template itself. The way WordPress templates work, there is usually a file called footer.php which controls the content displayed at the bottom of each page. While the placement of the code at the end of the page isn't absolutely required, it is a web design best practice.

To place the code into the template:

Locate the **footer.php** file.

Toward the end of the week, there should be a pair of lines:

</body> </html>

Create a new blank line above this line, then paste the script provided by Google into the new blank line.

NOTE: If you ever change to a different template, you must remember to re-insert the code into the new template.

ADDING GOOGLE ANALYTICS (GA) TO YOUR NON-BLOG WEBSITE

Adding GA code to any Web page is the same as steps two and three of the process for WordPress templates, except you must make sure that the code is included on every page that you want to track, and you will have to add them one at a time.

TRACKING MULTIPLE DOMAINS

Your GA account allows you to track multiple domains from one Google account. To add a domain to your Google analytics account, select "Create New Account" in the My Analytics Accounts drop down menu. From there, follow all of the steps for creating your first account. Note that the code that you will be inserting onto the pages will be slightly different.

UNDERSTANDING GOOGLE ANALYTICS REPORTS

After installing the Google Analytics tracking code into your blog (or website), you can log into your account's dashboard to monitor visitor activity. Here is a breakdown of the data provided in your Google Analytics dashboard:

1. Site Usage

This is where you can see the top-level stats of your website at a glance. How many total visits in the time period selected, total number of individual page views, pages per visit, bounce rate, average time visitors spend on your site, and the percentage of first time visitors to your site.

2. Visitors Overview

This is a repeat of the top level chart for daily counts of visitors.

3. Map Overlay

This area shows you geographically where your visitors are coming from. This can be especially useful for locating your fans.

4. Traffic Sources Overview

This chart shows from which sites visitors are reaching your site. If you notice a high percentage of visitors are coming from a particular area, you can focus your marketing efforts there.

5. Content Overview

This chart shows which pages within your site are getting the most attention. This information can be useful in deciding where to place important information, or what portions of your content are most interesting to your fans.

I. ANALYTICS: MEASURING YOUR EFFECTIVENESS

Analytics is the key to understanding your marketing effectiveness and your fan base. When you learn how to use analytics well, they will tell you what is working effectively versus what is not. The best part about analytics is you will know if your time and effort are making a difference.

We will give you four different services to try. The first is for social media, and the other three are music-specific. They all track your social media sites from one dashboard, and make the experience visually pleasing with charts and graphs.

1. Crowdbooster - http://www.crowdbooster.com

Crowdbooster is my favorite, free analytics app. It provides straight ahead, no-nonsense analytics in an easily digestible format. They show you when highly influential individuals (via Klout) follow you so you can make sure to engage with these fans.

For Twitter, Crowdbooster measures four main components: Impressions, Follower Growth, Influential Followers and Top Retweeters. Through graphs or tables (your choice), Crowdbooster will tell you how many impressions each of your tweets have. This app will identify your top retweeters. The interface also makes it easy to reciprocate by retweeting the users, which is key to tap into the larger follower bases.

For Facebook, analytics measure impressions, fan growth, and top fans. Much like Twitter, it's important to look at which posts are getting the most responses and continue to post similar status updates. It is important to adjust your strategy on posts that receive little to no feedback.

2. Music Metric - http://www.musicmetric.com

I hear a lot of great feedback about this UK-based analytics app. It's the least expensive of the three, starts at $15 per month and you get 15 days free.

4. Next Big Sound - http://www.nextbigsound.com

Next Big Sound also tracks all social media sites on your behalf and allows you to see where fans are based, so you can target your efforts. It also lets you look at other musicians so you can compare and contrast your activity with theirs. Next Big Sound is the most expensive of the three at $79 per month with 14 days free.

J. ARIEL'S SOUND TAKEAWAYS

- The key to your blogging strategy is consistency. If you commit to blogging, keep in mind that you should blog a minimum of twice a month

- Bloggers respect other bloggers, so adding blogging to your strategy is a fantastic way of setting yourself up to get covered on other people's blogs

- Commenting on blogs before you dive in and begin to write your own is a fantastic way of getting a feel for two-way conversations

- Indentify ten blogs and read them regularly and become a known contributor to them

- I recommend getting started with smaller blogs and not ones with huge amounts of traffic, if you want to be known in the community of that blog

- If you do decide to blog, vary your content and don't only blog about music

CHAPTER 6: *Pinterest*

A. ROOM FIVE IN YOUR SOCIAL MEDIA HOUSE

Pinteresting Facts

- Users of Pinterest spend more time on it then they do on Facebook

- Pinterest is now used by 15 percent of United States Internet users

- Pinterest was the fastest site ever to reach ten million monthly visitors

- Research indicates that Pinterest is more effective at driving traffic to websites than Google+, YouTube, Reddit, and LinkedIn combined

- Pinterest is used more by women (68%) than men (32%)

- An overwhelming majority of Pinners are between the ages of 25-54

- The average Pinterest user has 34 boards with close to 3,000 pins, following 300 other users

- Pinterest users' top interests include fashion, music art and memorabilia (this is fabulous news for musicians), quotes, and wine

- Pinterest is great for future money making! It is projected to account for 40 percent of all social media-driven purchases: Some say Facebook will fall to 60 percent, and Twitter will be nowhere

I added this fabulous newbie on the social media scene last, and it's "Room Five" because it is new compared to the other sites. Many musicians have told me they believe Pinterest is a lot easier to use than Twitter, because you don't need to think up anything clever in 140 characters, or bore people with the details of eating a sandwich. Pinterest is also less daunting than blogging, especially if you are a visual person; all you need to do is come up with themes and images that resonate with you.

B. PINTEREST IN A NUTSHELL

Pinterest is a social network that allows users to visually share and discover new interests by "pinning" images or videos to their own or others' "pinboards" (i.e. a collection of "pins," usually with a common theme).

You can link your Pinterest accounts to your Facebook and Twitter, so your pins can attract more eyes from different channels.

It's very easy to set up. Watch the following four-minute video from Blogging Bookshelf which will walk you through the Pinterest process.

MOVIE TIME!

Here is a movie to help you wrap your mind around Pinterest:

Pinterest in Four Minutes

http://bit.ly/PinterestIn4

C. HOW TO CREATE A PINTEREST ACCOUNT IN NINE STEPS

1. Visit Pinterest.com, and click "Join Pinterest."

2. You have an option to start your account from your already existing Twitter or Facebook accounts, or fill in all your information manually via email.

3. It will prompt you to follow five boards to get started. Pick boards that reflect your lifestyle, and ideas that you want to get across.

4. Activate your account

5. In the "Settings" tab in the right hand corner, change your company, or artist name as your username. Also enter your pitch into the description field, and your image to your headshot or logo.

6. Add your social media links!

7. Also make sure your "search privacy" feature is turned off, so that search engines can find your content.

8. You can add the "Pin It" button to your browser, to make it easier to pin interesting images that you come across on the web. You can also download an app for your phone. This option is located in the "About" tab in the upper right corner.

9. Start pinning!

D. FIVE EFFECTIVE MUSICIANS' PINTEREST PAGES

All of these pages have interesting boards – go see how the pros do it!

1. Britney Spears - http://pinterest.com/britneyspears

2. Katy Perry - http://pinterest.com/katyperry

3. Carli Munoz - http://pinterest.com/carlibistro

4. Yoko Ono - http://pinterest.com/yokoono

5. The Backstreet Boys - http://pinterest.com/backstreetboys

E. SEVEN STEPS TO ADD PINTEREST TO FACEBOOK

Woobox - http://www.woobox.com/pinterest

Woobox has a great Pinterest app that allows you to show your boards on your Facebook page by adding it as an app box (the boxes that appear under your timeline image). It displays your boards just as you laid them out on Pinterest, allows you to set a special board as a default, and gives you visitor analytics. The extra benefit here is you keep fans on your Facebook Fan Page instead of taking them to another social site.

1. Go to http://woobox.com/pinterest

2. Scroll all the way to the bottom and click "Get Started for Free."

3.This will take you to your Facebook page, with a popup. Click "Go to App."

4. It will then take you to a page to confirm that you would like to the pages associated with your Facebook account. Click yes to all.

5. You will then go to the page where you can view all tabs managed by Woobox. Click the Pinterest tab in the left hand column, and then clock "Add a Pinterest Tab."

6. Fill in the username info for your Pinterest account, then click "Save Settings"

7. You will now have a new tab installed on your Facebook Fan Page which will display all your Pinterest pins.

F. LUCKY 13:
13 PINTEREST BOARD IDEAS
FOR MUSICIANS

1. Locations (city you are from and places you tour)
2. Fashion and Style (what you wear on stage)
3. Musicians Who Influence You
4. Your Ultimate Studio
5. Your Favorite Era (70's, 60's etc.)
6. Favorite Quotes (throw your lyrics in here)
7. What Inspires You
8. Musical Instruments
9. Favorite Memorabilia/Tour Souvenirs
10. Charity/Causes
11. Your Brand (something that reinforces your brand)
12. Food, Drink, and Recipes (most commonly re-pinned)
13. Cute Animals (go viral!)

I look up to you sooo much!

thechive.com

G. CYBER PR®'S TOP PINTEREST APPS

Share As Image - http://shareasimage.com

This cool service lets you turn any quote or text anywhere online (hello – all of your lyrics!) and easily convert it into an image. It has two tiers: free and pro ($6.99). With the pro version, you can choose fonts, colors and text size. Once you've created your quote image, you can pin and share it.

Pinstamatic - http://pinstamatic.com

This is an incredible suite that contains many tools. My favorite tool allows you to pin Spotify tracks (see below). Pinstamatic also allows you to pin Twitter handles, create stickies, and add effects to photos.

H. ADDING MUSIC & VIDEOS TO YOUR PINBOARDS

It's easy to make your Pinboards musical!

SoundCloud - http://soundcloud.com

SoundCloud allows pinning. When you pin a track to Pinterest, its artwork pops up next to your other pins, and the SoundCloud player/widget will launch when the pin is clicked. You will always be credited because shared music is fully attributed, and links back to your artist page on SoundCloud. Read about it here: http://bit.ly/PinterestSoundcloud

Spotify - https://pinstamatic.com/#spotify

The Pinstamatic suite is very easy to use. My favorite thing is that it allows you to pin Spotify tracks. Just visit the following URL and enter your Spotify address: https://pinstamatic.com/#spotify and Voila!

YouTube - http://www.youtube.com

You can pin your YouTube video (and any) to your boards by installing the "pin it" button to your Web browser (works with Firefox and Chrome) and simply pin – or search for "How to Add YouTube videos to Pinterest" on YouTube and watch one of the fabulous many that pop up.

I. THREE WAYS TO TRACK ANALYTICS FOR PINTEREST

Google Analytics

Google Analytics works with Pinterest, so you can track how effective your Pinterest endeavors are.

The easiest way to do this in Google Analytics is with Referral Reports.

Go to "Traffic Sources > Sources > Referrals report." From there, if you don't see pinterest.com (or m.pinterest.com) in your top ten referrals, just use the inline filter at the top of the table to search for "pinterest" (hat tip to Mashable for this tip).

Pinreach - http://www.pinreach.com

Pinreach is like Klout for Pinterest. It measures analytics and influences metrics. It will score you based on a combination of activities, such as pin creation, repins, likes, and more.

Pingraphy - http://www.pingraphy.com

This app allows you to schedule pins to keep your fans engaged over time. It also helps you find influential users amongst your followers, and its metrics track repins, likes, clicks, and reach for every pin.

THREE KEY METRICS TO PAY ATTENTION TO:

1. Clicks Per Pin

- Will show the traffic referred back to your blog

- Must install Google Analytics on your blog

2. Re-Pins Per Pin

- Will show you internal Pinterest Analytics (Pins, Repins, Likes, etc.)

- http://pinreach.com

3. Average Visit Duration

- Find influential users among your followers

- http://pingraphy.com

J. SEE WHO IS PINNING YOU

In order to track what has been pinned on Pinterest from your website or blog, type the following URL into your browser:

http://www.pinterest.com/source/**YourWebsiteNameHere**.com

HAPPY PINNING!

Don't forget to come friend me at: http://pinterest.com/CyberPR.

K. ARIEL'S SOUND TAKEAWAYS

- Pinterest is about developing relationships with other pinners

- Diving in is the most important thing - start several boards, start pinning, and see what happens!

- Sharing music on Pinterest is still underexplored. See if you can build a group of pinners who will reshare your music

- Set up analytics so that you can track clicks back to your website or blog from Pinterest

- Pinterest is not just for women, even though they are still the largest demographic that use the site

- Find great artists' Pinterest sites and emulate them

- Follow artists and others that you admire

- Pin content from others in addition to original content

- Work to find the niches where you get most traction with your pins

CHAPTER 7:
Marketing & Newsletters

A. THE ROOF OF YOUR SOCIAL MEDIA HOUSE

Newsletter-ific Facts

- Email in 2013 has an ROI of $40 for $1 spent

- Topspin did a study of hundreds of artists which shows that 30% of all money that went into artist's pockets originated via email

- A Chadwick Martin and Bailey study showed that 86% of all survey respondents reported that they used email to share content, while only 40% reported using Facebook

- According to a MailChimp study of 200 million emails the top 3 words to avoid in your subject line are: Help, Percent off, and Reminder

- The same MailChimp study showed that including a recipient's first or last name doesn't improve open rates

- Many studies show that high quality newsletter lists will lead to high-quality responses and interaction

n this chapter I will dive into the roof of your social media house: a great newsletter. The goal is to give you all you need to be a pro at sending regular emails that your fans will want to open.

LONG STORY SHORT

Email is still king when it comes to generating revenue, specifically for musicians. You make relationships with fans on your social networks, and turn them into customers by driving them to sign up to your newsletter.

B. STUDIES PROVE

If you are still not sending regular newsletters, you should be.

Boston-based research firm, Chadwick Martin Bailey, completed a study that all musicians should know about. The biggest takeaway from this study is: If your audience skews older than 24, you better be starting an effective newsletter strategy now!

FOUR IMPORTANT HIGHLIGHTS

1. "Three-quarters of Web users are likely to share content with friends and family, and nearly half do so at least once a week. But while much social networking content is built around such shared items, most people still prefer to use email to pass along items of interest."

2. "Eight-six percent of survey respondents said they used email to share content, while just 49 percent said they used Facebook."

3. "Broken down by age, the preference for email is more pronounced as users get older. And only the youngest group polled, those ages 18 to 24, reverses the trend, with 76 percent sharing via Facebook, compared with 70 percent via email."

4. "Rather than focusing on sharing content they thought the recipients would find helpful or relevant (58%), most respondents cared more about what they thought was interesting or amusing (72%)."

Are you including content in your newsletters that is interesting and amusing? If you are just talking about your next show, or your next release, then you are missing the mark.

Recent studies by music marketing companies ReverbNation and Topspin have also proven that a newsletter is the primary way that artists are making money online.

Topspin's study has shown that 30 percent of their users' overall revenue was generated through their newsletters. Fans have a tendency to buy when they see a clear call to action in a newsletter. The sample in the data is comprised of a cross-section online marketing of campaigns they monitored, featuring many artists from different genres.

C. CHOOSING A NEWSLETTER PROVIDER

There are many reputable newsletter platforms available. Here are my three favorites:

1. FanBridge - http://bit.ly/FanBridgeInfo

If you want more control over the HTML design, the contact list itself, and so forth, I recommend FanBridge. It's very easy to import your existing contacts using an Excel file. They also make it possible to set up a "Fan Incentive," where fans can trade you their email addresses for a "free" Mp3 (a phenomenal way to accumulate contacts). It is also possible to update all of your Facebook and Twitter statuses from the FanBridge dashboard.

2. Nimbit - http://bit.ly/NimbitInfo

If you are looking for a one-stop-shop for both your newsletter and online commerce, Nimbit is the place. If you are ready to set storefronts on your home page or on Facebook, we would recommend looking into what they have to offer. Do be aware that they take a 20 percent cut of all transactions through their storefronts (fees of this type are fairly common).

3. ReverbNation - http://bit.ly/FanReachInfo

If you are already using ReverbNation, there is no reason to leave. They have a great service when it comes to newsletter management. They also have great widgets that may appeal to you. You can use it for full integration.

D. ELEVEN THINGS TO CONSIDER WHEN SENDING YOUR NEWSLETTER

1. Be Consistent – Send Newsletters at Least Once a Month

You should send your newsletters out consistently – and statistics prove that people are most likely to open their emails on Tuesdays and Wednesdays – so send on one of those two days, at around 12 noon. The reason for this is people often check mail from work, and they are swamped on Mondays (digging out from the weekend), and they are checked-out on Fridays.

A recent case study I read also suggests sending on Saturdays because people have time on weekends. The one downfall of this is that you may see a higher unsubscribe rate on a Saturday, but your open rates may indeed increase.

2. The WIIFM (What's in it for Me) Principle

People are constantly making decision in their lives based on what I call the WIIFM Principle. Whether they perceive it consciously or not, people are always thinking with this principle in mind.

As an artist, you need to provide new, potential fans with an incentive to sign up to your newsletter list. Unless they already adore you, they will not grant you permission to market to them unless you give them some sort of content in exchange for their email address.

3. Choose Your "From" Field Carefully

According to Doubleclick surveys, 60 percent of your readers determine whether to open your email based entirely on the "from" field. So choose this field carefully, and keep it consistent every month. Something generic may seem impersonal, like Newsletter@YourBand.com, so try putting your first name or first initial and last name there to personalize the address.

4. Keep Your Subject Line to 55 Characters

Most email programs cut off the subject line after 55 characters, so keep your subject line short and sweet, and to the point: five to six words max.

5. Get Personal

Saying something personal brings you closer to your fan base. So share a photo of something you love (your pet, your kids, your friends), or something fun and non-music-related you did recently, like a vacation.

6. Shorter is Sweeter

Remember, people have short attention spans. Keep the length of each of your newsletters short and sweet: four to five paragraphs max. If you have more content than that, link them to your blog via a hotlink, so interested people can read more.

7. You Don't Have to Have an Upcoming Show to Send a Newsletter!

How about inviting everyone on your newsletter out for drinks for an evening, or to join you for a show of another artist you love? Or share something fun that you've done recently; maybe you just purchased a new album and you love it, and you want to talk about it.

TIP: If you have shows to promote, keep your gig list short. If you have a long list of upcoming gigs, you don't want them to take up a large portion of the newsletter. Showcase a few, and then link fans to your site or Facebook Event page to find out more information.

8. Give Away a Free Gift or Make a Special Offer

For example, the first three people to respond get something: a free exclusive Mp3, something that you've done recently, like a special poster to one of your gigs, or a T-shirt. One of our artists, Pete Miser, actually held a contest for a pair of his old Adidas shoes! It was a great idea – he actually got his entire mailing list engaged, and one of his fans won a pair of his old sneakers. It was fun, and it was effective.

9. Mailing Address and Unsubscribe Link

Know that by law, you need to put your mailing address and an unsubscribe link at the bottom of each of your newsletters. If you are uncomfortable adding your home address, then open up a P.O. Box and use that. This is why using a newsletter provider is critical.

10. First Names Get Attention

Use your subscriber's name. The best way to get someone's attention is to include his or her first name in the subject line of an email, something like this: "Hey Peter! I've got news for you…" It's catchy, and it gets people's attention immediately to the subject of your email. Some email programs can allow you to customize your emails so that the first names of your email list appear in the subject line. Testing shows that the response rates will go up 50-70 percent or more if you include first names.

11. HTML is Better Than Text

Studies have shown that HTML emails get a better response than regular text emails. However, if you're dedicated to using all-text formats, keep your lines to 65 characters each. This way they will be formatted properly.

E. HOW TO WRITE AN ENGAGING NEWSLETTER

GREETING: MAKE IT PERSONAL

Share something non-music related in the greeting. Pull people in on a human level. Make them care about you as a person, not just as a musician.

Some ideas:

- Vacation

- Family time (doesn't need to be too specific)

- Whatever you are reading or listening to

- TV and movies you are into and why you liked them

Post photos of these personal touches on Instagram, Facebook, Pinterest, your blog, and so on.

GUTS: THE BODY OF THE NEWSLETTER

What are you up to as an artist? Are you in the studio? Are you touring? Writing new tracks? Remember, people love and connect to stories, so TELL STORIES!

GETTING: PUTTING READERS INTO ACTION

This Call to Action is the part of the newsletter that gets your fans to take action and it is the most critical part of the newsletter:

- Ask them to join you on Facebook, Twitter, Pinterest, etc.

- Ask them to vote for you in an online contest

- Ask them to review your CD on CD Baby, iTunes or Amazon

- Give them a survey to fill out or a contest to participate in

- Gift them a free download: A special gift makes you memorable

- Invite them to an upcoming show

TIP: There should only be one Call to Action per newsletter. Fans will get confused and choose nothing if they have more than one choice.

F. NEWSLETTER OUTLINE

HOW I STRUCTURE MY SOUND ADVICE NEWSLETTER:

1. Greeting

"In this issue" outlines what's coming in the newsletter.

1. Where's Ariel? DC and Denmark!

2. Feature Article: Your Social Media Pyramid

3. Have you joined the Blogging Challenge yet?

Next comes a "Hello!" And a quick summary of what I've been up to, or some other noteworthy company related news. Then, "Where's Ariel?" - which lists my upcoming speaking engagements.

2. Guts

Next I include my feature article.

3. Getting

I end with one Call to Action, such as:

- Follow Ariel on Twitter

- "Like" the Cyber PR® Facebook Page

- Purchase a copy of my book

EXAMPLES OF CALLS TO ACTION FOR COMMUNITY BUILDING:
(Try these before any Calls to Action for money)

- Follow you on Twitter

- Like your Facebook Fan Page

- Listen to a new track on SoundCloud

- Vote for you in any contest you may be in

- Comment on your blog

- Invite them out to hang with you at a bar, club, coffee house, another person's show, etc. This is great for bonding with them

- Have them watch a video of you on YouTube and subscribe to your YouTube channel

- Send them a survey to fill out or a contest to participate in.

- You could also simply ask them to have a free download – a special gift makes you memorable!

EXAMPLES OF CALLS TO ACTION FOR MONEY
(Once You've Developed Rapport)

- Invite them to an upcoming show

- Invite them to buy your music on iTunes, Bandcamp, or CD Baby: one track or a whole album

- Sell a merch item – a hat, a T-shirt, special item, etc.

- Let them know that you play backyard BBQs and private parties; have them email you if they are interested

- Record personalized songs upon request

TIP: Keep it short. If you've written a long newsletter, feature part of it in the newsletter, and then link readers to your website/blog for the rest. This is also a great way to draw traffic to your site or blog.

G. SURVEYS: HOW TO ASK YOUR FANS WHAT THEY WANT

The most successful marketers always test the waters before they release anything. A survey can help you create and launch a product line that caters directly to your fans. After all, it is your fans that will give you money and support your work. This could spell out the difference between you making a little money from your music versus making a lot of money.

CHANGING TIMES IN THE MUSIC BUSINESS

All of the current news surrounding the music business is bad news. Record industry veterans are getting laid off left and right and CD sales continue to drop as consumers get free music online. The ol' music business is still stuck in the same old pattern: "success" means selling one CD each to a million people (or many millions).

It's no longer sufficient to have only CDs and downloadable tracks for sale, because in your customer's mind there is little-to-no value attached to CDs and downloads (free downloads are readily available everywhere online).

This is an exciting time to come up with some alternatives and create some offerings for your core fan base that (in the long run) will make you a lot more money. It's time to break the mold and create something that is more sustainable for you as an artist.

NEW PARADIGM

The new paradigm should be a two-pronged approach:

1. Sell many things to a smaller group of your core people who know, love, and trust you. These core fans want to come back to you and to your brand many times over.

2. Create a sense of belonging and community around your music.

By doing this, your fans will feel like they are members of a club and not just buying a one-time thing.

HOW WILL YOU ACHIEVE THIS?

The first step is to build rapport with your email list. This comes down to communicating regularly and consistently with your fan base, and then, when the time is right, asking them for money.

Many artists I work with argue with me on this point and say that their fans get angry with them if they communicate using email too much.

Here's my take on this: if someone unsubscribes or requests to be removed, that's okay! Simply remove him or her from your list. People who ask to be removed from the list probably won't buy from you anyway, so remove them with joy and get on with bonding with the core fan base that wants to hear from you.

ASK YOUR FANS

Before you assume what your fans would like from you, we suggest that you conduct a free survey and ask them.

NOTE: If your list is small, you should focus on building it first. I consider a real fan base a minimum of 1,000, but a fan base of 5,000-10,000 is a great goal to work toward.

When preparing your survey, consider:

- What is your product line?

- Do you only sell CDs?

- Do you have merch or a fan club?

- How about a line of products that you can sell to your fans?

- Have you asked your fans what they are willing to buy, what they want, and how much they are willing to spend?

SURVEY TOOLS

Survey Monkey - http://www.surveymonkey.com

Survey Monkey is a great resource that enables you to create a free survey of up to 10 questions and send it around to your list for feedback.

Poll Daddy - http://polldaddy.com

Poll Daddy is another free resource for polls and surveys.

TwtPoll - http://twtpoll.com

TwtPoll is a great resource to ask questions, gain feedback, and engage your followers.

H. SEVEN TIPS TO GET FANS ONTO YOUR NEWSLETTER LIST

1. Add Friends and Family

Mine through your inbox and outbox. We all have them. Huge inboxes stuffed with email from people you're communicating with. Are they already on your email list? If not, email each of them and ask: Is it okay for me to add you to our newsletter mail list? (Be sure to offer a free Mp3.) If they say yes, add them directly onto your email list.

Create a separate folder in your inbox for potential email sign-ups and name it, "Newsletter Readers," and throughout the week, when you get an email from someone who you think would make a nice addition to the list, simply move them into that specific box. Then, when you have an hour, sit down to build your list.

TIP: Never, ever add someone without getting permission first, even if it's a friend, because that's considered SPAM.

2. Do a Live Giveaway/Raffle at Every Show

When you are playing a show, hold up a CD or a T-shirt on stage and announce you are doing a free giveaway and a raffle. Have a friend sweep through the venue with a hat and have all the people in attendance drop their business cards into the hat. When the hat reaches the stage, pull a random business card out and do a giveaway. Then, mention to the crowd that you're going to add everyone in the hat on your email list. You've just collected a ton of new email names and addresses that you definitely would not have captured otherwise.

3. Get Mobile - Start a Text Message List

Before you start playing a gig, when you are asking fans to switch off their cell phones, ask them first to text you their information. Then you build a mobile phone text email list and you can email people directly to their cell phones the next time you're coming through town.

TIP: You can also add to this list by putting a widget on your home page, inviting fans to opt in. This widget can also live on your website, Blog and Facebook Fan Page (more on this coming up in the mobile chapter).

4. Don't Forget Your CD Baby Sales Email Addresses

This is GOLD because this is a list of people who have already purchased your album. They are therefore ten times more likely to buy from you again! Go through your CD Baby sales and email every single person who has bought your CD with a personal note and sign them up!

5. List Trade With Another Band

Once you have a sizable email list, you can approach other bands that you play with or whose music is similar to yours (or maybe they're from your hometown), and you can ask them to write an endorsement email saying: "Hey, if you like us, you'll like our friends!" Then they can send that endorsement out with a request for joining your email list and you can, in turn, do the same for them. When you do a list trade with another band, always make sure that your music is very well described in a couple of sentences – what you sound like, who you get compared to – and if you can, take them directly to a page where they can get a free Mp3 that streams the moment they sign up so they can check you out.

6. Ask for Emails on Facebook and Twitter

For Facebook – Go to the personal profile of anyone that you regularly interact with on your Fan Page and send him or her a message asking for his/her email address. Always make sure it's personal (this will take some time but can yield golden results).

For Twitter – It is important to ask for an email address at the appropriate time. You wouldn't go up to someone you just met and immediately ask them for their phone number, would you? Once you have @ replied back and forth with someone multiple times, it's okay to direct message them, asking for their email address. Always assure them that their email address is safe with you, and that you will never sell it or give it to another party. You can also make periodic announcements on your Twitter stream offering incentives.

7. Use NoiseTrade

NoiseTrade is a platform for both artists and fans to discover each other. For the fan, it provides a fantastic and easy way to find new music. The fan is not obligated to pay for this music, but has the option of "tipping" you when they download the tracks and you get the gold (their email address and zip code).

Once a fan downloads the music, NoiseTrade provides social media links so the fan can quickly tweet about their download or post it to Facebook. If your new fan is really impressed (or feeling particularly guilty about their lack of monetary contribution), they can even get an embed code and install a widget on their website or social media profile, directing their friends to your music.

NoiseTrade has free widgets as well as opportunities to pay for promotions. Visit them here to find out more: http://noisetrade.com

I. ARIEL'S SOUND TAKEAWAYS

- Your newsletter doesn't have to be perfect the first time - just send it out and improve upon it each time

- Don't just fill your newsletter with news and information about your band's activities - include "fun" information that will get your fans excited

- The key to the success of any great band, company or project starts with the size of its list; start building your list!

- Add people to your list carefully; make sure they have opted in to receive your newsletter

- Read your newsletter and think about how you would respond if it came to your inbox every week?

- Once you have built a solid newsletter, reach out to different communities, perhaps through NoiseTrade or another program

- Have fun with it! Your fans will notice

CHAPTER 8: *Google*

A. THE SUN SHINING ABOVE YOUR SOCIAL MEDIA HOUSE

Some Google-icious Facts

- Google is the number-one ranked website

- Google gets over four billion hits per day

- Gmail has around half a billion users

- Gmail gets sign-ups from over 5,000 different establishments, companies and businesses every day

- Every day, the Google +1 button is used more than five billion times

- 2/3 of Google+ users are male

Google, in my humble opinion, is the most amazing invention I can think of. Google is not just a big search engine (although it would still be awesome if that's all it did). Google has been offering a suite of incredibly powerful tools for years, way before "in the cloud" became the next big thing for companies like Apple and Microsoft as well. What's more, Google has also created a platform for musicians that offers tools that will help musicians all over the world thrive in the digital realm.

B. EIGHT USEFUL GOOGLE TOOLS

1. Google Alerts

Have you ever spent hours trying to track down articles on your band or a certain topic? With Google Alerts, whatever words, phrases or terms you select will be searched by Google and emails of all of the found articles and mentions will be delivered to your inbox.

To Setup A Google Alert: Visit http://www.google.com/alerts

- First, choose your search terms. You may include wild card characters (*) to expand the search to find words containing the search terms

- Use quotation marks (" Cyber PR ") to search for only the exact words in the search, in the exact order entered

- Choose the type of alert you would like

- Select the frequency of alert emails (Daily works best)

- Enter the email to which you would like the alerts emailed

2. Google Blog Search

This is basically a filter for only searching blogs, and with 200 million blogs out there, on top of all the websites, this is a great filter for all the noise. This is also a great place to track your band on blogs. To search on Google's Blog search, go to this link: http://blogsearch.google.com

3. Gmail

If you still have an AOL, Yahoo!, or Hotmail address, you're in trouble. Gmail just may be the best email program on the planet. Many bloggers and new media makers use Gmail and it shows you're in the know, so get signed up. Google email is wonderful because it is searchable by topic or by word, and Google provides you with a huge amount of storage space.

Also, when you use Gmail as your default mail host, you can set up a custom URL through GoDaddy, then point it to Google's server, and *voila!,* you have a customized email address.

4. Google Drive

Google Drive is like the entire Microsoft Office Suite for free. It's synced completely online so you can access it from anywhere without taking up any storage space on your computer, and can also be shared with anyone who has a Google account. This is a helpful tool for you and your team to keep track of lyrics, merchandise, accounting, and anything else, for which you would otherwise have to use often-expensive word processing programs such as Microsoft Word or Excel.

5. Google Music Artist Hub

In November 2011, Google introduced its first digital music store, called Google Music. Unlike iTunes and Amazon, Google Music has made it easy for you to get your music listed for sale by creating the Google Music Artist Hub, a platform for you to list, organize, and manage all of your music being sold in their store. To make it even better, having your music for sale in the Google Music store also means that you can sell your music though YouTube as well!

All you need to do to get on Google Music is to register for an Artist Hub account, which requires a one-time, $25 fee, and they will walk you through how to get your music published!

Visit this link for the details: https://play.google.com/artists

6. Google Calendar

Google Calendar is a highly integrated, yet simple calendar application that is synced to your Google account so it can be accessed from anywhere you can access the Internet. The best reason for you to be using Google Calendar is that multiple users can sync to the same calendar. It is a free solution for you, your band, and your team to be on the same page for any upcoming events or deadlines that you have.

7. Google+

Google introduced Google+ (pronounced "Google Plus") in June 2011, and the Facebook-meets-Twitter design and functionality made it the latest and greatest social networking platform to enter the competitive market. What makes Google+ so important for you is that it is a Google owned and operated platform, therefore it ranks very highly in Google searches, helping with your search engine optimization. It is also measured in Klout, so if you care about your Klout score, get +1ing and posting.

8. Android

Google has entered the mobile market with Android, which is now the most widely used and fastest growing mobile operating system available. The obvious benefit to using Android is that it syncs all of your Google apps together, including Google+, Gmail, Google Reader, Google Calendar, Google Music and even Google Drive, so that you'll never miss a beat when you're on the go.

C. GOOGLE+

In June 2011, Google introduced their own social networking platform with the intention of entering the ring to contend for the social media crown against the likes of Facebook and Twitter. This platform, simply dubbed Google+, showcases quite a few similar features as its leading competition.

As an artist, you may be asking yourself, "Why would I even bother if I'm already on Facebook and Twitter? Do I really need to update yet another social media account?"

Frankly, the answer is yes, you really do need to get yourself set up on Google+ and the reasons are quite simple.

WHY MUSICIANS CAN'T AVOID GOOGLE+

1. Google+ pages rank very highly (if not #1) in Google searches

This is incredibly important for any emerging musician trying to establish an online presence, as it will almost instantly increase your visibility. Even if you are still too obscure for your Facebook Fan Page or your personal website to appear towards the top of a Google search, a Google+ page will almost instantly rank towards the very top.

2. Google+ is the fastest growing social network in history

Of course it is! Google is already such a dominant force that anything they introduce can grow, and fast. So it is no surprise that Google+, introduced in June of 2011, received 20 million visits in the first 21 days of its existence. If Google+ can continue to grow at its current rate, it may be able to give Facebook a real run for its money.

3. Google+ has already shown to be a powerful tool for musicians

Within the first weeks of the Google+ launch, a singer/songwriter named Daria Musk took advantage of some of the FREE Google+ features, namely Google Hangouts, to host a virtual concert to hundreds of fans and new listeners.

MOVIE TIME!

In the Cyber PR® Web series, *Sound Advice*, Team Cyber PR® and I did a two-part interview with the amazing Google+ pioneer Daria Musk on how she used the platform to rocket her career to the next level. Watch them here:

> **Part I** - http://bit.ly/DariaGoogle1
>
> **Part II** - http://bit.ly/DariaGoogle2

THE FEATURES

Whether or not Google+ is the most wildly original social network since the dawn of the Web isn't important. What is important is that Google+ is here to stay, and should be an important platform and marketing tool to consider, when creating a strategy to build your online presence and influence.

The following are five of the most important features that you, as a musician, need to know about in order to make the most of the time and effort you put into Google+.

1. Band Pages

The quintessential feature that you must be familiar with is Band Pages. A Google+ Band Page is a page that you can make, just like a Facebook Fan Page, that caters directly to musicians.

It is crucial that you sign up for a Band Page as soon as possible so that you can solidify the URL and Band Page name to remain consistent with the rest of your social presence. This process is very simple:

- Once you sign up for a Google+ account, you will see a link to "create a page" on the right side bar towards the bottom of your profile.

- From here, all you need to do is select the "Arts, Entertainment and Sports" option and create the page!

It is truly that easy and will make a HUGE difference in your overall online visibility. Of course, you want to make sure you complete your Google+ Band Page with bio, and high-resolution pictures of yourself or your band. Unfortunately at this point in time, Google+ Band Pages still don't have a way for you to upload music directly to the page, so you'll want to use this page primarily to engage your fans.

2. Circles

Google+ Circles are THE core function of the website and it is how Google+ positioned itself as a unique competitor in the social networking market.

As far as you need to be concerned, Circles are really just lists. Google+ functions similarly to Twitter in that you can simply follow anyone you'd like without needing their approval by adding them to a Circle. The main benefit is that you can create separate Circles for all of the different people and resources you need to stay on top of.

Here are some Circle ideas I suggest you create to start:

- Your Super Fans

- Venues

- Similar Bands/Bands that Influence You

- Fans (Create a new Circle for each major market or region where your fans exist. Great for upcoming show promotions!)

- Blogs that you follow

- Music Industry Resources

- People who make you laugh

- Your Best Friends

3. Hangout

As mentioned above, singer/songwriter Daria Musk was able to utilize Google Hangouts to host a virtual concert for hundreds (and eventually thousands) of fans and listeners within her first three sessions! So what is Google Hangout?

Simply put, Google Hangouts is a free and easy to use video conferencing service similar to Skype (actually, Facebook's introduction of Skype video chatting was a response to Google+'s introduction of Hangouts).

The reason this service is so important for emerging musicians is because it allows you expand the face-to-face time with fans to beyond just live events.

4. Photos

I know what you're thinking ... More photos?

Well, yes. More photos. But thankfully Google+ has made it far easier than any other platform to upload photos directly to your profile! When Google+ was originally introduced, Google also released the Google+ mobile apps for the iPhone and Android operating systems. Within these apps, there is a fantastic function that allows the app to automatically upload all pictures taken from your phone directly to your profile. Yes this will drain more battery from your smartphone, but I think it's worth it to know that every photo you take, be it from the recording studio, from the road, or even from an awesome new restaurant, is now a piece of content that you can share with your fans.

5. Google +1 Button

When Google+ was launched, the +1 button became its integrated engagement marketing tool. This button (like the "FB Like" and the "Tweet it" buttons), allows anyone to "+1" any page and add a comment. Encouraging people to press this button helps your Google+ profile rank higher in Google searches.

So what does this mean you may be asking? Well, it doesn't mean much in terms of how you use Google+, but it does mean that the +1 Button is now an absolute must, along with the Facebook Like button, on your website and blog! Including this will turn your website into an easily sharable, highly visible site on Google+.

As an emerging musician, it's critical that you stay on top of the evolving trends of social media so that you can properly maintain and grow your online presence. This ultimately leads to a bigger, more dedicated fan base. Google+ is the latest, major introduction into the social media world and it's important to stay on top of it, so you don't fall behind other artists who are adapting.

D. ARIEL'S SOUND TAKEAWAYS

- Google is so much more than email and search

- Use Google Drive to streamline shared docs with your entire team and never send docs by email again

- Google Calendar is also a great tool for sharing things that a team needs to coordinate on

- Use Google Blog Search to find blogs that will cover you

- Use Google Alerts and never have to search for relevant things - they will come to you

- G+ is now integrated with all of Gmail and it's worth updating often - cross post your blogs and share articles frequently (and don't forget to look at comments)

- Search out the +1 button and share things you like often

- Keep your Google Profile updated as it shows up in places you may not realize

CHAPTER 9: *Mobile*

A. THE CHIMNEY OF YOUR SOCIAL MEDIA HOUSE
Text-worthy mobile stats

- Of 200 million Twitter users, 60% log in via mobile once per month

- 70 percent of iPhone and Android users visit Facebook on their phones

- Mobile Internet usage will overtake desktop Internet usage by 2014

- Mobile coupons get ten times the redemption rate of regular coupons

- Three out of five Internet searches are done with a mobile device

- 91 percent of mobile Internet access is used for socializing

- Smartphones are in use by over half of consumers in the U.S.

I have taken you through a whirlwind tour of social media throughout this book so far. But we are not done yet. I believe a huge part of the future of marketing lies in Mobile. If your Social Media House starts with a solid foundation, the front door, and then five rooms, Mobile is the chimney.

Winter is coming. If you don't keep yourself warm, you're going to perish. If you already have most of your house in order, the most important thing is to dive into mobile, and warm yourself by the fire.

DO YOU CONSIDER YOURSELF MOBILE-SAVVY?

I'm not just talking about texting. I'm talking about using your smartphone to tap into and enhance your online presence while staying up-to-date on all of the cool apps that are designed to make your life a little easier. Pay attention! This is where social media is headed.

B. START AT YOUR FRONT DOOR

Remember when I said your website is your front door? We need to go all the way back there to begin your mobile strategy. The size and technological restrictions of mobile Web browsers may make your "perfect" website look completely off-putting if accessed from a phone. And you want to make sure your site is not the victim of such a mobile tragedy.

So, just how important is it to make sure your fans have the proper website experience from their smartphones? A stunning new study from Nielsen came out recently, which reveals that in March 2012, smartphones were in use by 50.4 percent of all phone consumers in the U.S. This means, many of your fans will fit into this 50.4 percent.

There is a huge opportunity for you to get your message and your voice directly into people's pockets. It's called the third screen in "marketing speak." (The first screen is your TV, your computer is the second, and your mobile phone is the third.)

BEGIN EMBRACING YOUR MOBILE STRATEGY AS SOON AS POSSIBLE

Pull up your website onto your smartphone (or use a friend's if you are not in the 50 percent). Ask yourself, "How does it look? Is it navigable?"

Put yourself in your fans' shoes. The three most important assets that should be immediately accessible are:

1. Access to your Facebook Fan Page

2. Access to your Twitter (or YouTube or both if you create videos for your promotion)

3. Information about live appearances/tour dates (if you have them)

TIP: On the day of every live appearance, make sure you create updates and tweets with the time of the show and venue address via Twitter and Facebook (in case a fan on the way to your gig is trying to access this information).

YOUR WEBSITE SHOULD BE OPTIMIZED FOR MOBILE BROWSING

Ask your Web developer to make sure he or she can handle this task, or test it yourself from a few different types and makes of devices, as all are different.

TIP: Flash players for your music are not compatible with Apple devices (iPhones, iPads or iPod Touches), so avoid having a Flash player for your music. I highly recommend using SoundCloud.com as your player instead. It works on all hand-held devices.

MOVIE TIME!

One of the leading app developers for bands and musicians, Mobile Roadie, just released the following two videos which are chock full of interesting facts and figures about the state of the mobile world today.

Listen to key tech and music industry voices — including Topspin, Last FM, The Orchard, PIAS Media, Sound Exchange, Media Temple, Yahoo, Echo Nest and Mobile Roadie as they discuss the future of mobile tech and audience engagement. Shot at SXSW 2012.

Part I: Evolving Beyond The Web

http://tinyurl.com/beyond-the-web (I'm featured in the video)

Part II: Rethinking Fan Engagement

http://tinyurl.com/fan-engagement

C. THE POWER OF TEXTING

Mobile marketing has been around for a while, but many still are not taking advantage of it because they're not quite sure how. Text messaging is a very powerful way to capture and engage fans.

It is effective because people tend to have their phones with them at all times. How can you effectively reach out to your fans and let them know you have a last minute / surprise show tonight? The same way you would reach out to any of your friends: with a text!

D. MOBILE APPS

It is critical for your website to be mobile-ready, so that all your fans that try to view your website and blog while on-the-go are able to do so! However, there is another option that is available for all of you that is worth considering: an app! While mobile Web browsing has become increasingly popular, the use of apps is the most effective and intriguing part of smartphones.

By creating your own personalized app, you can give your fans an easy to use and powerful experience that includes all of the capabilities of a fully-functional website without taking your fans out of their regular mobile routines.

There are several affordable app building services that you can explore. Each offers different features, including:

- An HTML-5 based platform that works across all smartphone platforms (iOS, Android, Blackberry)

- Analytics tools so you can see how many fans are using your app and from where

- Content syncing that will allow you to update all of your social networks from one place

- Location based push notifications

- A store/ marketplace

E. MOBILE APPS FOR MUSICIANS

Listed below are the most popular app-building platforms used by independent musicians. Each offers a similar service with a slightly different look and feel. Ultimately, the one you choose will come down to which look and feel connects best with what you are trying to accomplish.

2. Mobile Roadie

Mobile Roadie allows you to create an app, integrate your social media profiles, track app users, and market it through QR codes, pop-ups, push messages, and more. Mobile Roadie has a free website option, but prices increase with added features.

BONUS: Mobile Roadie also has a free site builder that will allow you to not only have an app, but also an HTML-5 based, mobile-ready website for fans who haven't yet downloaded the app.

3. Mobbase

Mobbase is an app that allows fans to download a pseudo-VPK (Virtual Press Kit) right to their phones. Mobbase allows you to stay connected with your fans by posting your music, news, photos, videos, store, discography, blog, and more. Their more advanced (and costly) options allow you to post your app on to the iTunes App Store and Android Market.

4. ReverbNation

ReverbNation has a free/inexpensive solution for creating a mobile app in only six easy steps! This app allows you to upload photos, include your bio, and upload links to your social media sites and blog. ReverbNation's app creator hosts your app for both Android and Apple Products.

F. SEVEN MOBILE APPS MUSICIANS NEED NOW!

New apps are being introduced every day and companies are always finding new ways to make just about anything possible from your phone. If you're ready to simplify your life and amplify your fan interactions (mostly for free), then get your smartphone out and check out these seven apps:

1. Square / Cost: FREE

Let's say you just played a show, and you've got a newly converted fan that absolutely can't get enough of you. She loves your music so much that she wants to buy five CDs – one for her, and the rest for some family and friends. Awesome, right? One problem, though – she only brought her credit card. Well, that's a bummer. How are you going to scan her card without some sort of card reader? Oh, wait, do you have a smartphone? Then consider your problem solved!

Square is a fabulous app that allows you to swipe any credit card and deposit the money into your bank account. Once you sign up on the website, they'll send you your free card reader. Then just download the app and set everything up, and you'll never have to worry about the "cash-only" dilemma again!

2. Tweetbot / Cost: $2.99

Twitter is one of the easiest ways to keep up with your network in real time while you're out on the road. While Twitter does have its own app, many find it somewhat lacking. For a Twitter app with a little personality and some cool features, why don't you try Tweetbot?

Tweetbot lets you read and create tweets (of course,) but there's more! You can create lists of different types of people, such as co-workers or fans by location, and view timelines of only their tweets. You can also read a whole conversation thread with a single swipe of your finger, and customize the app so you can use it however you'd like best.

3. Facebook Pages Manager / Cost: FREE

Make sure you're staying on top of your page with the Facebook Pages Manager. Let everyone know what you're up to, scroll through your news feed, upload your cool photos easily, and check into your favorite coffee shop! You can pretty much do anything you could normally do with Facebook, right on your phone.

4. Instagram / Cost: FREE

Think you're a good photographer? With Instagram's effects, you could even "wow" yourself. And with photos acting as one of the most well-received and popular kinds of Facebook updates, there's no reason not to post them more often!

Instagram provides a smooth, easy, and great-looking interface to snap pictures with your phone, add different filters to transform them, and share them easily with your social networks. Warning: it can be addictive!

5. Dragon Dictation / Cost: FREE

Okay, so you're out getting some lunch with your buddies, and suddenly… inspiration hits. You saw or heard something, and you got a cool idea for some new song lyrics. But you're in the middle of lunch, so what do you do? Quick – just record your voice!

To record your voice and turn it into text with surprising accuracy, give the Dragon Dictation app a shot. You can even use it to write emails, which could be especially helpful if you aren't the world's fastest texter.

6. Smartr / Cost: FREE

This amazing app, which you can plugin to your Gmail account through the app store, or add to your phone, shows you your Facebook, Twitter, and LinkedIn profiles. It also includes your email history for each of your contacts, showing your communication and even the subject of your very first note. Its the perfect app for staying interconnected across your social media sites - and it will even automatically follow everyone in your email on Twitter in one click (if their email matches their Twitter email).

7. SendHub / Cost: FREE

SendHub is a service that allows you to send texts to groups of people, and they've just released a mobile app. Just sign up on the website with your mobile number and download the app to use the site easily from your phone. SendHub provides you with a unique number, so your real number can stay private. Anyone can subscribe to your group texts by texting the group's keyword to your SendHub number, and can unsubscribe by texting "STOP." The app lets you create your groups right out of your iPhone contact list and manage your account on the go! A free account gets you up to 1,000 messages per month and up to three groups, with 50 numbers max per group.

G. REAP THE BENEFITS

Mobile is a necessity for artists of any level. While you may not be ready for a custom app from Mobile Roadie, everyone needs a mobile-ready site. Plus, everyone can reap the benefits from the mobile tools outlined in this chapter.

Building your mobile presence and brand can seem like a daunting task at first, but it only takes a few simple steps to create an integrated, pleasant experience for your fans. Mobile provides more immediate access to your fans, on both the micro and macro levels, than we've ever experienced in the past.

Embrace the mobile revolution and you WILL reap the benefits.

H. ARIEL'S SOUND TAKEAWAYS

- Your website must be mobile friendly - you'd be amazed at how many people are browsing it on their phones

- Experiment with making group text messaging lists for friends and fans in each city you tour in (if you store them in your phone)

- Smartr - If you have a smart phone - make it as smart as can be and use it to make all contacts interconnected using Smartr

- Square is the most amazing way to instantly accept credit cards (with authorization) on the road!

- If you have a large enough base a mobile app can be a dynamic way of interacting with fans

CONCLUSION

A. GETTING INTO ACTION

really want this book to make a difference for you. But it won't if it becomes a "shelf-help" book and not a self-help book. Many of you may read this entire book, but you will not implement what you see on the pages. Others are perfectionists and feel they need to read the whole thing cover to cover because they want to wrap their head around the concepts first and see what they are getting into (sound familiar?) Then, because these perfectionists are overwhelmed by implementing the whole thing *perfectly*, they do nothing. (Don't be that perfectionist ... Get to work!) Some of you will read the whole book and find it interesting in theory, but will feel frozen because it's just too much.

My advice is, if you are the type who has read this whole book so far, and you are now sitting there in a state of overwhelm, pick just one thing from the following list, and just commit to doing that one thing. Even if you just do that one thing well, it will make all the difference.

- Identify Your Niches

- Your Website

- Facebook

- Twitter

- YouTube

- Blog

- Pinterest

- Newsletters

- Mobile Strategy

B. GIVE YOURSELF A SOCIAL MEDIA ASSESSMENT

The Cyber PR® Social Media Analysis Process

Facebook Fan Page

- Is there a Fan Page or only a Personal Page?

- If the artist has both are the posts different on each profile?

- How many fans?

- How many people talking about the page?

- Is the timeline banner image high quality and consistent with artist's overall branding?

- Is there a high-quality profile image?

- Is there an 'about' section below the profile image that contains a strong elevator pitch line and link to website?

- Have the 4 'apps' buttons below the timeline banner been optimized so that 'likes' button removed, all apps are relevant, functional and look good? (Note that there should only be 1 'artist page' type app on the page - if there are 2, please say so.

- Is the full about section optimized with a proper bio, links, etc?

- Is there a post every day?

- Is the content varied in the forms of media (photos, videos, links, text. etc.)?

- Is the content being posted in a way that encourages engagement (i.e. asking questions?)?

- Is the content overly self-promotional (more than 1 in every 4 posts is self promotional)?

- Is there a common theme being used throughout the content?
- Is there a newsletter sign up?

Twitter

- How many followers?
- How many following?
- Is the homepage skinned?
- Is the page skinning / profile image the same or consistent with Facebook?
- Is there a strong description? Does it match the one on Facebook?
- Is there a link to the homepage (URL) on the bio?
- How many tweets per day?
- Is the content tweeted varied (links, videos, images, etc.)?
- Is the content overly self-promotional? (More than 1 in every 10 tweets is self-promotional)
- Is the artist engaging others with RTs, #MM and #FF or using any hash tags on a consistent basis?

YouTube

- Do the Social URLS Match (Twitter, Facebook, etc.)
- Is the page skinning/ profile image the same or consistent with Facebook?
- Is there a strong description? Does it match the one on Facebook
- How many subscribers?
- How many views?
- How many videos uploaded?
- How often are videos being published?

- Are videos published with proper titles, descriptions, and tags?

- Are there more tan 7-8 tags per video

- Are the comments being answered or addressed

Blog

- Is the look and feel consistent with Facebook and Twitter?

- How often are posts being published? Are they consistently published? (Should be at LEAST one time per month)

- Is there an overall theme to the posts?

- Do the blog posts have any comments on them?

- Is there a newsletter sign up widget or form included?

- Is there a special free offer when you sign up for the mailing list?

- Are there links to the artist's socials (Facebook, Twitter, YouTube, Pinterest, etc.)?

- Is the blog easy to locate from the homepage?

- Is it EASY to comment (no captcha, no signup to the site to comment)

- Are there any comments at all – what are your observations of them?

Pinterest

- Is there an account?

- Is there a clear bio with a pitch?

- Are there links to other sites?

- Name of account - does it match the other socials

- Followers / following

- Are there any Likes? (Should be many)

- How many boards? Should be at least eight

- How many pins on each board? Should be at least 15 – 30

- Is there any self-promotion (merch items, links back to artists site etc.)?

- Is Pinterest included on other socials (FB, Blog etc.)?

C. ATTACK PLAN

To help you spring into action, I have put together this bulleted attack plan so you can work your way down the list and implement!

ROOM ONE: FACEBOOK

- Outline your desires, angles, news, updates and content strategy (remember to diversify your content and NOT just self promote).

- Optimize your Facebook Fan Page & Personal Page (if you use it for promotion) to more effectively brand, and market to your customer base and obtain deeper engagement.

- Create relevant status updates for your Fan Page and interact with fans on your behalf. Cross populate blog posts and Tweets.

- Monitor Insights (analytics) to make sure status updates are posted at optimal times, e.g. when followers are most active and responsive.

- Strategize on special opportunities such as contests, newsletter sign up drives, E for M (email for media), or similar widgets and charity tie-ins.

USE SPOTIFY

- Create an Artist Spotify user account and Playlists, and update

Playlist content regularly – share on your Facebook page and ask fans to contribute.

- Regularly promote your Playlist through Facebook (Personal Page – if you interact with fans here).

- Send out personal messages via Spotify to everyone who subscribes to the Playlist for relationship building.

- Make a submission to the Spotify App "Sharemyplaylist."

ROOM TWO: TWITTER

- Think about your tweet angles, news, updates and content strategy (mix it up!).

- Add hundreds of new followers each month – find people you like and see who follows them then run down the list and follow all (don't think!).

- Tweet updates based on your personal interests, and angles (charities, politics, hobbies, etc.).

- Ensure followers are engaged with you by sending @'s, RTs, and DM's.

- Use Crowdbooster.com to monitor analytics to make sure tweets go out at the optimal times, e.g. when followers are most active and responsive.

- Crowdbooster.com will also monitor when influential individuals follow you and make sure you are engaging them – make it a goal to reach out to three per week.

- Strategize special opportunities such as contests, newsletter sign-up drives and charity tie-ins and share your music!

ROOM THREE: YOUTUBE

- Go over your desires, angles, news, updates, and come up with a content strategy to create content (i.e will you need to hire a videographer etc.) and calls to action

- Drive views to your channel by cross-populating your videos onto your Twitter, Facebook, and blog

- Engage all of your new followers and ensure that you are following, subscribing and having two-way conversations when they leave comments

- Strategize special opportunities such as contests, newsletter sign-up widget and charity tie-ins

ROOM FOUR: BLOGGING

- Schedule a monthly strategy session with yourself to organize and integrate your likes, interests, and unique story so that your online voice and brand gets communicated effectively on your blog

- Create ideas that you want to blog about that are relevant, consistent, and tie in with your overall brand and message

- Ask your fans to write fun guest posts to add on a biweekly or monthly basis (depending on desired strategy)

- Drive views to your blog by cross posting bit.ly links onto your Twitter and Facebook pages and pin them on Pinterest

ROOM FIVE: PINTEREST

- Pinterest is retaining and engaging users as much as two to three times as efficiently as Twitter. According to AppData and Facebook, a large majority of Pinterest users are women. So if women are in your desired target group, USE this fab platform!

- Engage with potential fans on this addictive platform but repin what they post, repin at least 10 images a week

- Watch how the PROS do it and copy:

  Britney Spears: http://pinterest.com/britneyspears
  Yoko Ono: http://pinterest.com/yokoono
  The Backstreet Boys: http://pinterest.com/backstreetboys

- Create boards (at LEAST 10) and make them FUN
- Integrate with your Facebook page and talk about your pin activity on your blog

HERE'S TO YOUR SUCCESS!

APPENDICES

APPENDIX A:
20 CRITICAL WEB 2.0 SITES FOR MUSICIANS

Facebook, YouTube, Twitter & Pinterest are not here, but that's because you are already on all four of these, RIGHT? Here are 20 More Sites You Should Know About (and use!).

1. 15-Second Pitch

15secondpitch.com helps you craft, write, and fully define your 15-second elevator pitch. The pitch wizard on this site walks you through a step-by-step process to create it and this site makes you more Google-icious because it ranks high in that mighty search engine.

2. Amazon

Amazon.com is a great place to create a profile that will be found in Google. On it you can curate lists of books, music, or products you really like as well as review albums and books you enjoy. You can also ask your fans to review your music on Amazon for more overall traction on the site.

3. Artist Data / Sonicbids

Socicbids.com is a great way to present your press kit and it's a necessity if you want to submit to music festivals like SXSW and CMJ, and they now own Artistdata.com, which helps you publish tour date information to a variety of destinations online from one single dashboard.

4. Bandpage

Bandpage.com (used to be called Root Music) is a free app for adding music to your Facebook Fan Page and across the net. Bandpage not only allows a music player and buy links to be added but it also lets you skin your Facebook Fan Page so that the whole look and feel of it matches your branding and colors.

5. Bandzoogle, Bombplates & Hostbaby

If you want a slick looking website and you don't want to pay a lot for it, I highly recommend all three: Bandzoogle.com, Bombplates.com, and Hostbaby.com. They all have many beautiful templates to fit your brand, and customer support is wonderful to deal with.

6. Bit.ly

Bit.ly is a link-shortening site that helps you take long URLs that you may want to share with your community and makes them small (so you can fit them into tweets and Facebook status updates). The best part is, it reports how many clicks and retweets you receive for each bit.ly you create.

7. Blogging Platforms

WordPress, Blogger, & Tumblr are three fast and easy sites where you can set up a blog, choose a theme, and be off to the races blogging for free and in less that 10 minutes. A Web designer can incorporate all three of these sites easily into your own site.

8. Fan Funding Platforms Pledge, Rockethub, Indiegogo & Kickstarter

Okay, I know this is actually four sites not one, but fan funding is such an important aspect to the artists career in the new music business, I did not want to single out just one platform. Each has its differences, but all help you to raise money from your fans for whatever you want to use it for.

9. Fanbridge

Fanbridge.com - If you do not have a newsletter management system in place, and you are not sending newsletters regularly and consistently, look to Fanbridge. Their interface is easy to use and their analytics and articles are amazing, so you can educate yourself on best practices and measure your results.

10. Foursquare

Foursquare.com is another free app that prompts you to check in when you are out and about. It's kind of like a human video game as you receive badges and points for checking in to places that have them, and now thanks to some great partnerships, you can be rewarded with discounts, coupons, and free stuff!

11. Hootsuite

Hootsuite.com is a Twitter management tool that helps you to see tweets based on lists, keywords, or hashtags. It will help you schedule tweets and manage multiple accounts elegantly.

12. Hype Machine

Hypem.com is an Mp3 and music blog aggregator that scans over 4,500 blogs each day and shows you the most popular songs and posts about music on the Web - search and discover something new and if you want to get the attention of respected music bloggers, start reading (and commenting on) featured blogs from the Hype M network.

13. Instagram

Instagram.com is a photo app owned by Facebook that makes it ridiculously easy to share and edit photos by choosing cool filters and fun tools to edit. It is free and available for free in the Apple App Store and Google Play store.

14. Jango

Jango.com is an online radio service that functions like Pandora (you can curate whatever type of station you would like to listen to). However, Jango has a twist: You can buy spins on it and tell Jango which artists you would like to be played alongside. Listeners have an opportunity to give you direct feedback and even share their email addresses with you.

15. Klout

Klout.com measures your influence on your social networks. It tracks your activity and engagement on Facebook, Twitter, Linkedin, and Foursquare and measures your influence based on your ability to drive action such as likes, follows and comments. You should know your Klout score.

16. Last.fm

Last.fm is a wonderful Internet radio site where you can create a profile (or update one) that friends and fans have already created for you.

Create your own Last.fm stations and tune into personalized radio. Scrobbling a song means that when you listen to it, the name of the song is sent to Last.fm and added to your music profile. Songs you listen to will also appear on your Last.fm profile page for others to see.

17. Music Think Tank / Hypebot

Musicthinktank.com / Hypebot.com – Music Think Tank is a group blog that brings together ideas and thoughts from tastemakers in the online music business. MTT is run by Hypebot.com, which is a great resource for all news that is music industry related.

18. Nimbit

Nimbit.com is a suite of great tools that can help you do many things including send and monitor your email newsletters, build an affordable WordPress site, streamline your social media and establish a store to sell your music and merch right on your Facebook Fan Page.

19. ReverbNation

ReverbNation.com is an amazing site designed to empower artists with marketing tools. The deep stats and information they provide about your fan base will help you make decisions on where to market, tour, and grow your business. Use them for email management and for my favorite widget for collecting emails in exchange for songs: http://tinyurl.com/reverbfreebribe

20. Twitpic/YFrog

Twitpic.com and Yfrog.com both allow you to use your mobile phone to snap pictures and easily upload them to your Twitter account right as links on your tweetstream. This will also show up to your Facebook if you have them connected.

APPENDIX B:
CYBER PR® ONLINE TERMS DICTIONARY

API (short for Application Protocol Interface): is how Web applications interact with one another. You may hear people referring to sites as having "Open APIs." This means programmers are welcome to build onto them to interact with them (Such as Twitter).

Avatar: The graphic representation of a person online. It is typically used to help the person navigate a virtual world. Some try to make their avatars look like themselves, and others go for idealized/stylized visions.

Blog: A Blog is really just an informal website. Blog sites are online journals or diaries that are usually more personal and more subjective than a proper website.

Blogosphere: The collective countless blogs on the Web (think atmosphere). There are currently over 80 million blogs online.

Cloud Computing: Cloud computing is a service rather than a tangible product, and it is the process by which shared resources, software, and information are provided to computers and other devices over a network (the Internet). Examples include Google Drive and Spotify.

CPC (Cost Per Click): the sum paid by an advertiser to search engines and other Internet publishers for a single click on their advertisement which directs one visitor to the advertiser's website

CPA (Cost Per Acquisition): the amount paid to publishers per each piece of information collected (in this case, email addresses)

CTR (Click-Through Rate): the percentage of people who click a link they are presented, as in an online ad (this is a useful definition for you when you are buying Facebook Ads)

Embed: a way to include a snippet of code (usually some sort of digital media or widget) from one site onto a Web page somewhere else on the Internet

Folksonomy: A group of people working together to organize information into categories.

HTML: This term stands for "Hyper Text Markup Language." It is a language used to develop and create Web pages.

Hyperlink: A graphic or word that opens another document when you click on it. Hyperlinks are the main way to navigate between different websites and between individual pages within one website.

Internet Radio Station: Listening to radio broadcasts via the Internet using streaming techniques. The audio is played via a software media player or a browser plug-in that supports streaming audio formats such as those from RealNetworks and Microsoft. Internet radio may be streamed at the same time as live AM and FM broadcasts over the air, or it may be a recording of a previous broadcast. In the latter case, selecting the station again after it started will reset the stream to the beginning.

Keyword: A keyword is the term used for words included in a Web page that match words used by people searching the Web (like in Google). Keywords can simply be words included in the body text of the document, or added to the header using meta tags to increase the number of keywords (your web designer can easily do this). Selecting keywords, that match your target audience's use of the Web is a critical marketing tactic. (definethat.com)

Mashup: A Web service/software tool that joins two or more tools in order to create a whole new service. The term is also used to describe user-generated remixes of content from multiple sources.

Newsgroup: A virtual area online reserved for the discussion of a particular topic.

Newsreader: This service gathers the news from multiple blogs or news sites via RSS so that readers can access news from a single website or program.

Opt-In: A direct, voluntary request by an individual email recipient to have their email address added to a specific mailing list.

Opt-Out: An email subscription practice that allows users that request it to be deleted from an email distribution list by either selecting a link or sending an email that requests their address be deleted.

Plugin: A software component that adds to the functionality of WordPress. This component "plugs into" the application.

Podcast: A podcast (at its core) is an audio file that is created along with some code that enables the file to be downloaded to your computer, where it can be streamed in a player or downloaded to a portable player. There are now thousands of free podcasts available online and at iTunes.

Podsafe: Podsafe is a term created in the podcasting community to refer to any work which, through its licensing, specifically allows the use of the work in podcasting, regardless of restrictions the same work might have in other realms (Wikipedia).

RSS: RSS stands for "Really Simple Syndication" and is a Web feed format used to publish frequently updated content such as blog entries, news headlines, or podcasts. RSS solves a problem for people who regularly use the Web. It allows you to stay informed easily by retrieving the latest content from the sites you are interested in. You save time by not needing to visit each site individually. You ensure your privacy by not needing to join each site's email newsletter. The number of sites offering RSS feeds is growing rapidly and includes big names.

RSS Reader / Feed Reader: RSS content can be read using software called a "feed reader" or an "aggregator". The user subscribes to a feed by entering the feed's link into the reader or by clicking an RSS icon in a browser that initiates the subscription process.

Tagging: A tag is a (relevant) keyword or term associated with or assigned to a piece of information (e.g. a picture, article, or video clip), thus describing the item. Tags are usually chosen informally and personally by the author/creator or the consumer of the item. Tags are typically used for resources such as computer files, Web pages, digital images, and Internet bookmarks (both in social bookmarking services, and in the current generation of web browsers). (Wikipedia).

Server: A computer that houses websites and is connected to the Internet 24-hours per day.

Social Bookmarking: The ability to save and categorize a personal collection of Internet bookmarks and share them with others. Users can also take bookmarks saved by others and add them to their own collection or subscribe to others' lists.

Social Media: Online technologies that people use to share opinions, experiences, insights, and perspectives with each other.

Social Networking: Websites that make it possible for people to link to others to share opinions, insights, experiences, and perspectives. The people sharing these ideas might be friends on Facebook, business contacts on LinkedIn, classmates on Facebook, etc. Many media sites have now incorporated social networking features such as blogs, message boards, podcasts, and wikis to help build online communities related to their content.

Streaming Media: Video or audio transmitted over a network that plays immediately when users click on it, without the need for a file download. RealMedia, QuickTime, and Windows Media are the most common streaming formats.

Tags: Keywords attached to photos or Web pages to help identify them and allow them to be logged by Google and other search engines.

URL: This term stands for "Uniform Resource Locator." It is a string that supplies the Internet address of a website or page on the Internet.

Viral Marketing: Any marketing technique that gets websites or users to pass on a marketing message to others.

Viral Video: Video content (usually humorous in nature) that has become popular by sharing, usually via email or media sharing websites.

Vlog: Video-based journals (like blogs) that are posted online.

Web 3.0: The evolution of Web usage and interaction along several separate paths. The process by which the Web has been transformed into a database as well as its movement towards making content accessible by multiple non-browser applications.

Webcasting: Communicating to multiple computers at the same time over Internet by "streaming" live audio and/or live video.

Webisode: A short video that can only be found on the Web.

Widget: A third-party item that can be embedded in a Web page.

Ariel Hyatt

Ariel is a recognized thought leader in the digital PR world. Her groundbreaking PR methods - coupled with her vast experience as an esteemed new media educator - enable her to effectively and accessibly initiate her clients into the ever-growing world of digital PR. She started her business (which later turned into Cyber PR®) when she was 23 years old, and has a message to share with young people aspiring to work in the music industry: It is possible. She has been honored to speak at The Clive Davis Institute of Recorded Music at NYU, Belmont, MTSU, University of Colorado, Drexel University, City College, Fordham, Borough of Manhattan Community College, Cape Breton University, William Paterson University, and Berklee College of Music. She looks forward to adding many more to the list.

Ariel's game-changing work has been lauded by industry professionals and highly established media outlets alike, garnering her press in CNN, Wired, Billboard, Hypebot, and The Washington Post. Her message is so compelling, she has been invited to speak at festivals and conferences in twelve countries, including SXSW, CMJ, ASCAP's I Create Music, The Future of Music, Grammy Camp, The Taxi Road Rally, The New Music Seminar, The 140 Conference and over 60 more. She lives in Brooklyn with her gray tabby Hunter C. Thompson (the C. stands for cat).

TWITTER @CyberPR

FACEBOOK http://www.facebook.com/CyberPR

TEACHER'S GUIDE
CYBER PR®
FOR MUSICIANS

CHARLIE B. DAHAN, A. RICHARD MEITIN WITH ARIEL HYATT

TOOLS, TRICKS & TACTICS FOR BUILDING YOUR
SOCIAL MEDIA HOUSE

Cyber PR® for Musicians Teacher's Guide

Renowned music industry professors Charlie Dahan and Richard Meitin have collaborated on a systematic classroom guide that simplifies social media for students of all levels. Through exploring the innovative approaches in digital PR insider Ariel Hyatt's book Cyber PR® for Musicians, Dahan and Meitin have written a text that enables instructors to turn newbies into pros in one semester.

Book Includes:
- Step by step guide to Hyatt's "Social Media House" principles.
- Thoughtfully organized chapters that correspond to the student's text, Cyber PR® for Musicians.
- Quizzes, group assignments, and questions for discussion based on each chapter's main theme.

"Charlie Dahan and Richard Meitin are well-suited to guide how educators should teach digital PR. Between the two of them there is vast experience throughout the music industry and in teaching environments, and they have taken Ariel Hyatt's concepts and aptly brought them into this Teacher's Guide for Cyber PR® courses."

Jeffrey Rabhan — *Chair of the Clive Davis Institute of Recorded Music at New York University's Tisch School of the Arts.*

"As a member of The Collective - Nashville's management team -I work with digital media every single day and I can definitely attribute the beginning of my education in that field to Cyber PR®."

Rachel Cunningham — *Student, Middle Tennessee State University*

Call Cyber PR® to order the Teacher's Guide: (212) 239-8384, or order online at the following URL: http://www.cyberprmusic.com/education.

MUSIC SUCCESS

IN **9** WEEKS 🐦

A STEP-BY-STEP
GUIDE TO SUPER
CHARGE YOUR
SOCIAL MEDIA &
PR, BUILD YOUR
FAN BASE, AND
EARN MORE
MONEY

by Ariel Hyatt

3RD EDITION

Music Success in 9 Weeks

Music Success in 9 Weeks is a guide for musicians to define their brand, grow their fan base, earn more income, and achieve success in the digital environment, whether they are new to the industry or long time artists. Music Success in 9 Weeks provides the missing manual for musicians trying to make sense of the social media revolution and explains step-by-step how to create a profitable and sustainable business for their music. This book can easily be deemed the "what to do next" bible for both new and established artists.

Structured like a workbook, with room for exercises and notes, the book takes all of the guess work out of where to start and how to achieve success as a musician in today's world.

"You need to buy this book, now! It's the only one that directly answers: 'I've got great music, but now what?' Read it, and you'll be earning its value back ten-fold."

Derek Sivers — *Founder, CD Baby*

"How good is this book? I figured that I would just skim through the book since I already know a good bit about how the social media world works, but I couldn't put it down and wound up learning a lot about myself since the book covers so much more than social media. Her information is concise, to the point, and easy to grasp, no matter if you're a social media veteran or just dipping your toe into the online waters for the first time."

Bobby Owsinski — *Author, Music 3.0*

"Music Success in 9 Weeks is a top pick for those who want their chance at the big time."

Midwest Book Review

Cyber PR® Certification Exam

One of the most exciting parts of creating The Cyber PR® courses at MTSU was being able to offer a tangible asset that the students could take away from their experiences learning from us.

Charlie Dahan (co-author of the Teacher's Guide to this book) and I are both "TopSpin Certified" and we thought that TopSpin's idea of creating a certification process is cutting edge for a fractured music business, where there really are no marketing standards. It is very useful for artists, managers or labels looking for agencies who understand how to execute using TopSpin's toolsuite. Therefore agencies who could tout that they were "TopSpin Certified" added cache to their offerings.

The Cyber PR® Certification Exam is intended to do the same thing: Create a standard that potential employers can understand and give the student marketing practitioner a real leg up and a fabulous asset to add to their resumes.

A Cyber PR® Certification says: I understand the new rules of marketing, PR, social media and Two-Way engagement and their importance when promoting artists.

It was our wish that the students would opt to take this certification – and many of them have.

Our TopSpin students have gone on to land full time jobs in the business and many of them say it was the Cyber PR® Class and the real world experience that helped to get them to understand the "Full Picture" using tools they used every day in the "real world" and with real artists not just hypothetical case studies.

Both Charlie and I are thrilled that the result yielded full time jobs.

If you are interested in administering or taking the Cyber PR® Certification Exam please contact us. We would be thrilled and honored to arrange it.

Rock On!!

ARIEL HYATT, Founder of Cyber PR®
Email: ariel@cyberprmusic.com
Telephone: (212) 239-8384

CPSIA information can be obtained at www.ICGtesting.com
Printed in the USA
BVOW10s1245010514

352132BV00009B/221/P